THE CONVERSATIONAL WORD
OF GOD

This book is Number 8 in

Series IV: Study Aids on Jesuit Topics

THOMAS H. CLANCY, S.J.

THE CONVERSATIONAL WORD OF GOD

A Commentary on the
Doctrine of St. Ignatius of Loyola
concerning Spiritual Conversation,
with Four Early Jesuit Texts

THE INSTITUTE OF JESUIT SOURCES
St. Louis, 1978

IMPRIMI POTEST: Very Reverend Leo F. Weber, S.J.
Provincial of the Missouri Province
April 6, 1978

IMPRIMATUR: Most Reverend John N. Wurm, S.T.D. Ph. D.
Vicar General of St. Louis
April 20, 1978

TABLE OF CONTENTS

*Published through the aid of funds
donated by the late Mr. James L. Monaghan
of Milwaukee, Wisconsin,
1867-1963,
in memory of his brother,
Reverend Edward V. Monaghan, S.J.,
1879-1922.*

EDITOR'S FOREWORD

Simple and friendly conversation about spiritual topics, with individuals or groups, was one of the chief means of apostolic ministry employed by St. Ignatius of Loyola (1491-1556) and his companions who joined him in founding the Society of Jesus; and this procedure penetrated and undergirded all the other more visible activities to which the success of these first Jesuits is often attributed, such as preaching to crowds, giving the Spiritual Exercises, or organizing men and institutions.

That is the fact of history, all too easily overlooked, which Father Thomas H. Clancy develops in the present short book. It is a scholarly study, well documented from early Jesuit writings, but expressed in a pleasant chatty manner which makes it more readable and fruitful for personal reflections. The Institute of Jesuit Sources is happy to publish it as a monograph in its Series IV, Study Aids on Jesuit Topics.

It seems advisable to state the rationale of Series IV in each volume published in it. The series is an effort to solve various aspects, different from book to book, of the following problem.

From its inception the Institute of Jesuit Sources has been oriented toward publishing books of quality in both scholarship and manufacture. Such books, carefully selected and usually rather long, obviously have advantages—especially the long-lasting values arising from their presence in libraries. But this orientation, if maintained exclusively, also entails two disadvantages in our present era of rapid developments and changes: the lengthy time required for the meticulous writing and editing, and the corresponding expense of the finished clothbound volumes.

There is, however, another class of writings, such as doctoral dissertations, study aids, bibliographies, monographs, preliminary editions, and documented or well-founded reflections, which have a different but genuine value. These are, in many cases, not yet the finished, polished, and fully matured scholarship ordinarily found in the volumes published by university presses. But they are a firm step toward such scholarship. They contain much sound material which is truly helpful to interested persons and which would remain unavailable if postponed until high perfection could be attained. In many cases such delay could all too easily turn out to be an instance in which the dreamed-of best, which may never come, is the enemy which defeats the presently attainable good.

This Series IV consists of studies in this category. Hopefully, too, it offers some solution of the problem sketched above. An effort will be made to keep the books or booklets inexpensive, often through the use of typewriter composition and paper bindings. Editorial time and cost, too, will be kept as low as possible, with the responsibility for details being allowed to rest more fully on the authors than on the editors of the Institute of Jesuit Sources.

In the designing of this new series, many helpful ideas have been taken from the somewhat similar procedure in scholarly publishing which has been launched by the Council on the Study of Religion, for example, in the two "Dissertation Series" respectively of the American Academy of Religion and of the Society of Biblical Literature. The rationale of these series is well described by Robert W. Funk and Robert A. Spivey in the *Bulletin for the Council on the Study of Religion*, Volume IV, number 3 (June, 1973), pages 3-13, 28-29, and 36-37; and also, at greater length, in the *Report of the Task Force on Scholarly Communication and Publication*, edited by George W. MacRae, S.J. (1972, available from the Council on the Study of Religion Executive Office, Waterloo Lutheran University, Waterloo, Ontario, Canada). Indebtedness to this helpful information and example is gratefully acknowledged.

George E. Ganss, S.J., Director
The Institute of Jesuit Sources
Easter, 1978

AUTHOR'S PREFACE

My interest in the topic of spiritual conversation was aroused by an article of Maurice Giuliani, fed by a suggestion from William Byron, and encouraged by the enthusiasm of Michael Mendizabal. I also profited from conversations, in part spiritual, with Georges Bottereau, at the time the librarian of the Jesuit Generalate in Rome, where most of the translations were made and the first draft of this study was written. The translations are very free indeed. I aimed for something like the tone of Today's English Version of the Scriptures and took the same liberties with the text that characterizes that translation. The originals are easily available to the scholar and should be consulted.

This manuscript was finished before I discovered the doctoral thesis of Darío Restrepo, written under the direction of Michel de Certeau at the Institut Catholique in Paris in 1971. Father Restrepo has since reworked his material into an excellent book, *Diálogo: Comunión en el Espíritu.*[1] This work, however, treats the matter from an entirely different viewpoint emphasizing spiritual conversation in religious governance, whereas my perspective is that of the conversation of an apostle in his work.

All the gentlemen named above are Jesuit priests, but none of them are responsible for the shortcomings of the present work. I have based myself on early Jesuit teaching in what follows. But just as other facets of Ignatian teaching on prayer and the apostolate have proved helpful to Christians at large, it is hoped that the lessons St. Ignatius gave to his followers will enrich the apostolate of all preachers of the word, especially the lay preachers. With the permission of Loyola University Press, Chicago, the translations of St. Ignatius' Letters are from *Letters of St. Ignatius of Loyola:* Selected and Translated

---

1 Darío Restrepo Londoño, S. J., *Diálogo: comunión en el Espíritu. La "conversación espiritual" según San Ignacio de Loyola (1521-1556),* (Bogotá: Centro Ignaciano de Reflexión y Ejercicios, 1975). The author has condensed his key ideas into *Communications,* No. 6, " 'Spiritual Conversation' according to St. Ignatius of Loyola," 23 pages (St. Louis: The Institute of Jesuit Sources, 1976).

by William J. Young, S.J. (1959); and the versions of the Autobiography are from Young's *St. Ignatius' Own Story as Told to Luis González de Cámara* (1968).

> Thomas H. Clancy, S.J.
> St. Charles College
> Grand Coteau, Louisiana
> Feast of Our Lady of Guadalupe
> December 12, 1977

THE CONVERSATIONAL WORD
OF GOD

ABBREVIATIONS

used in the footnotes

Autobiog — *The Autobiography of St. Ignatius.* There is a critical edition in *FN*, I, 353-507. Of the two recent editions in English, *St. Ignatius' Own Story*, trans. by Wm. J. Young, S.J. (Chicago, 1968) and *The Autobiography of St. Ignatius Loyola* ed. by John C. Olin (New York, 1974), only the former has the very helpful paragraph numbers inserted by the editors of *FN* in MHSJ.

Cons — *The Constitutions of the Society of Jesus.*

ConsSJComm — *The Constitutions of the Society of Jesus. Translated, with an Introduction and a Commentary*, by George E. Ganss, S.J.

Da Câmara — Luis Gonçalves, *Memoriale*, critical edition in *FN*, I, 527-752. There is a French version by Roger Tandonnet, S.J. (Paris, 1966).

EppIgn — *S. Ignatii Epistolae...et Instructiones*, 12 volumes in MHSJ.

FN — *Fontes narrativi de Sancto Ignatio*, 4 volumes in MHSJ.

LettersIgn — *Letters of St. Ignatius*, translated by William J. Young, S.J. (Chicago, 1959).

MHSJ — Monumenta historica Societatis Jesu (Madrid from 1894, Rome from 1929).

MonFabri — *Fabri Monumenta*, vol. 48 of MHSJ (Madrid, 1914). This contains Favre's *Memoriale*, but a more critical text, not yet published, is the basis of Michel de Certeau's French translation (Paris, 1960).

MonNad — *Monumenta Nadal*, vols. 13, 15, 21, 27, 90 of MHSJ.

PolCompl — *Polanci Complementa*. Letters and notes by Ignatius' secretary, vols. 52 & 54 of MHSJ (Madrid, 1916-1917).

SdeSI — *Scripta de Sancto Ignatio*, vols. 25 & 26 in MHSJ.

SPIRITUAL CONVERSATION AS A MINISTRY OF THE WORD OF GOD

Spiritual conversation is one of those topics that is so evident that no one writes about it. It rarely merits a book, an article, or even a place in the index of most works of spirituality. Some spiritual writers teach that spiritual conversation is a means of encouragement and advancement for those who are gifted with mystical prayer. Thus St. Teresa of Avila counsels, "I would advise those who give themselves to prayer, particularly at first, to form friendships and converse familiarly with others who are doing the same thing...." She speaks of the encouragement she received from her conversations with St. Peter of Alcántara. "He delighted in conversing with me. To a person whom our Lord has raised to this state, there is no pleasure or comfort equal to that of meeting with another whom our Lord has begun to raise in the same way."[1]

At the very beginning of his conversion Ignatius of Loyola discovered the same truth. He went on, however, to develop spiritual conversation as a means of the apostolate, as a ministry of the word of God. For him spiritual conversation was a privileged means of preaching the good news. When he lists in his *Constitutions of the Society of Jesus* the means of helping one's neighbor, he starts with good example and then deals with prayers and holy desires, the administration of the sacraments, sermons and instruction in Christian doctrine both inside and outside of church, and finally, "...They will endeavor to be profitable to individuals by spiritual conversa-

---

1 See the Life of the Holy Mother Teresa of Jesus, chs. 7 and 30, in *The Complete Works of St. Teresa of Jesus*, trans. and ed. by E. Allison Peers, I, respectively pp. 37, 194; also, Poulain, *The Graces of Interior Prayer* (London, 1950), p. 146. Ignatius of Loyola has similar remarks in some of his letters of spiritua' direction. See, e.g., *LettersIgn*, pp. 69, 180.

tions, by counselling and exhorting to good works, and by conducting Spiritual Exercises" ([648]).²

Any discussion today of the ministry of the word of God is inevitably influenced by the developments which have occurred in biblical and kerygmatic theology in the last few decades. We used to speak of "preaching" the gospel. Now we are apt to think more in terms of "proclaiming" or "heralding" the gospel. The new terminology is frequently used in the decrees of the Second Vatican Council. In the very opening sentence of the decree on revelation we find: "Hearing the word of God with reverence and proclaiming it confidently, this most Sacred Synod...."³

The notion of the minister of the word of God as a herald who proclaims the word of God surely conveys better than the old terminology the action of the prophets of the Old Testament who professed to be nothing more than the mouth of Yahweh, and who proclaimed His word with little regard for time or place or the disposition of the audience.

It is easy too to see how John the Baptist fits into the line of the prophets.

> In the fifteenth year of the reign of Tiberius Caesar,...the word of God came to John son of Zechariah in the desert. He went about the entire region of the Jordan proclaiming a baptism of repentance....⁴

Right after he recounts the proclamation of the Baptist, Luke continues with what appears to be intended as the triumphal inauguration of Jesus' preaching.

> He came to Nazareth where he had been reared, and entering the synagogue on the sabbath as was his custom, he stood up to do the reading. When the book of the prophet Isaiah was handed him, he unrolled the scroll and found the place where it was written:

---

2 Numbers in square brackets refer to the marginal numbers of the Jesuit Constitutions written by St. Ignatius. See *The Constitutions of the Society of Jesus, Translated, with an Introduction and a Commentary*, by George E. Ganss, S. J. (St. Louis, 1970), hereafter abbreviated *ConsSJComm.*

3 Walter Abbott, S. J., ed.: *The Documents of Vatican II* (New York, 1966), p. 111.

4 Luke 3:1-4. My translation.

4

'the spirit of the Lord is upon me;
    because he has anointed me.
He has sent me to bring the Good News to the poor,
    to proclaim liberty to captives,
recovery of sight to the blind
    and release to prisoners,
    to announce a year of favor from the Lord.'

Rolling up the scroll he gave it back to the attendant and sat down. All in the synagogue had their eyes fixed on him. And he began by saying to them, 'Today this Scripture passage has been fulfilled in your hearing.'[5]

In that sense Jesus simply presents the divine revelation to those who had come to worship in the synagogue. There is little effort on his part to persuade or to lead them gradually to a deeper realization of God's purposes, such as he will do later, for example, to the disciples on the road to Emmaus and to the apostles all during his public life.

In fact the overwhelming impression that one gets from the Gospels is that relatively few of Christ's words were "proclaimed." We see him preaching, and he impressed the people with his power and authority as a teacher. But most of the words we read in the Gospels are portrayed as conversational rather than declamatory. He spends a good deal of time dealing with individuals or with small groups. He is a teacher rather than a preacher, and there seems to be a very conscious pedagogical effort on his part. This is perhaps most evident in the Gospel of John, which at times appears to be nothing more than a series of one-on-one encounters of Jesus with Andrew, Peter, Mary, Nicodemus, the Samaritan woman, the man born blind, and many others.[6]

Of course, the words of Jesus were never considered by the Christian community to be as important as his deeds; and it is these that really constitute the Good News and are emphasized in the primitive Christian kerygma. But even in the formulation of the Gospel his *pedagogic* method comes through—"He went about doing good."[7]

5 Luke 4:16-21. My translation.
6 "This Gospel is above all the Gospel of encounters and dialogues with Christ," Donatien Mollat, S. J., "St. John's Gospel and the Exercises of St. Ignatius," in *Communications*, No. 5 (Oct., 1975).
7 Acts 10:38. My translation.

The people of God have always drawn inspiration from this more intimate side of Jesus and have perhaps been more attracted to Jesus, the good shepherd, than to Jesus, the prophet of YHWH. The Second Vatican Council speaks in several places of the duty of proclaiming God's word, but it recognizes that this can be done from other places than the pulpit. It exhorts pastors to know their people individually and praises the ministry of religious, who teach doctrine, encourage through exhortation, give in simplicity, and console through cheerfulness. Truly, "the ministry of the word is carried out in many ways. . . ."[8]

Every Christian is supposed to be a missionary, a person who conveys the Good News of Christ to the world. The only way most Christians can fulfill this obligation is by godly conversation. And even the clerics among us who are authorized to proclaim the gospel from the pulpit will never reach the vast majority of mankind in this manner. Ignatius discovered this in his own life and valued spiritual conversation from the beginning of his conversion as a means of spreading the gospel.

In 1539 after a group decision to form a particular kind of religious order, Ignatius of Loyola had drawn up a statement of their basic purpose known as the "First Sketch of the Institute of the Society of Jesus." Slightly revised, this statement was incorporated in the papal bull, *Regimini militantis Ecclesiae* (1540), which approved the Society of Jesus as a religious institute. With further revisions, rather slight, the statement received its final form in another papal bull, *Exposcit Debitum*, issued by Julius III in 1550. It came to be known as the Formula of the Institute. Predating as it did any Jesuit rules or constitutions, this Formula occupies a privileged place as the most fundamental charter of the new religious order.[9] The second and third sentences are devoted to the works of the Jesuits.

---

8 Abbot, *Documents of Vatican II*, p. 540; see also pp. 419, 472.
9 Ganss, *ConsSJComm*, p. 36. The text of the Formula is given ibid., pp. 66-72. There is a useful collation of the successive versions of the Formula by Mario Gioia, S. J., in *Introducción al Estudio de la Fórmula del Instituto S. I.*, (Rome: Centrum Ignatianum Spiritualitatis, 1974), pp. 75-100.

He is a member of a Society founded chiefly for this purpose: to strive especially for the defense and propagation of the faith and for the progress of souls in Christian life and doctrine, by means of public preaching, lectures and *any other ministration whatsoever of the word of God*, and further by means of the Spiritual Exercises, the education of children and unlettered persons in Christianity, and the spiritual consolation of Christ's faithful through hearing confessions and administering the other sacraments. Moreover, this Society should show itself no less useful in reconciling the estranged, in holily assisting and serving those who are found in prisons or hospitals, and indeed in performing any other works of charity, according to what will seem expedient for the glory of God and the common good.

In the last years of Ignatius' life one of his closest collaborators was Jerónimo Nadal. His chief occupation under Ignatius and for some years later was to promulgate and propound the Constitutions of the new Society among its rapidly growing membership. His intimate contact with Ignatius and his early companions made him a privileged witness to the true spirit of the Jesuits. In several exhortations he undertakes an explanation of the Formula. His firm opinion was that the chief ministry designated by the phrase "any other ministration whatsoever of the word of God (*aliud quodcumque verbi Dei ministerium*)" was the ministry of spiritual conversation.[10] In him, as in Peter Canisius and Ignatius of Loyola himself, there is a consistent and integrated doctrine of his ministry and the means to become proficient in it.

10 *MonNad*, V, 665.

Chapter 2

SPIRITUAL CONVERSATION AMONG THE EARLY JESUITS

The founder of the doctrine was Ignatius. He was not converted by preaching but by the reading of the lives of Christ and the Saints. In the early days of his conversion he felt a strong need for spiritual conversation.

> At this time he still spoke occasionally with a few spiritual persons who had some regard for him and liked to talk with him. For although he had no knowledge of spiritual things, he showed much fervor in his talk and a great desire to go forward in the service of God.[1]

His method is worthy of note. He never shouted the good news from the housetops except figuratively. His tone was conversational. In Spain he used to engage one or more pious women in talk about godly things in the courtyard of a hospital or a chapel. It was as if he was telling them a secret, and years later a witness testified that though he tried to eavesdrop he could not understand what Ignatius was saying. But Ignatius got marvelous results. A witness tells us that even at Manresa right after his conversion there were women who "followed him day and night eager to hear the exhortations and spiritual words which he never tired of speaking to them."[2]

It is evident that we have something more here than what Teresa of Avila refers to in the passages cited above. These conversations were not principally aimed at sustaining a tiro in the spiritual life and enabling him to persevere in prayer. They were genuine attempts to aid souls. And this desire to

---

1 *Autobiog*, ch. 3, nos. 21, 34, trans. by W. J. Young, S. J., in *St. Ignatius' Own Story* (Chicago, 1956), p. 18.

2 *SdeSI*, II, 85. See Maurice Giuliani, S. J., "Qu'attendait Saint Ignace des Exercises?" in *Christus*, no. 10 (1956), esp. pp. 175-176. In his *Autobiog*, ch. 3, no. 28, Ignatius confesses that he could not stop speaking about the Holy Trinity.

share with others the insights he had gained into God's goodness flowed from his prayer. Polanco, one of Ignatius' earliest biographers, wrote of his discovery of the divine truths which later formed the *Spiritual Exercises*. "...And because they [these divine truths] had a great effect in his soul he wanted to assist others by means of them. And he always had these desires to communicate to others what God had given him, finding by experience that not only did he not lose what he shared with others, but his store actually grew."[3]

This desire to aid souls, which was born of Ignatius' first mystical experience, found two principal outlets both in Manresa and throughout his life: spiritual conversation and the corporal works of mercy, chiefly helping the poor and the sick. Later on at Salamanca the Dominicans were doubtful of his orthodoxy. They asked him and his companions, "What do you preach?" Ignatius answered, "We do not preach but we do speak familiarly of spiritual things with some people, as one does after dinner, with those who invite us."[4]

We do not hear of Ignatius preaching in the conventional manner many times in his life. When he revisited his native town of Azpeitia in Spain in 1535, he lived in a hospital where he engaged those who came to see him in godly conversation. He preached also in the parish church on Sundays and feast days and once to an open-air crowd from a tree, but most of his ministry consisted of conversation and catechism.[5]

Later that year he came to Venice where "he busied himself giving the exercises and in other spiritual conversations"[6] for more than a year. We also hear of him preaching in northern Italy in 1537 but by the testimony of his companions, though he was convinced he was preaching in Italian, his sermons were a strange mixture of Latin, Spanish, and French; and most of his preaching was done in the street where he attracted a crowd by waving his hat and held their attention more by his

---

3 Javier Osuna, S. J., trans. by N. King, S. J., *Friends in the Lord* (London: The Way, 1974), p. 12.

4 *Autobiog*, ch. 6, no. 65.

5 Ibid., ch. 9, nos. 88 ff.

6 Ibid., ch. 10, no. 92, trans. by J. F. O'Callaghan in *The Autobiography of St. Ignatius Loyola* (New York, 1974), p. 86.

saintly fervor than his eloquent words.[7] The following year he preached a few sermons in Spanish in Rome.

We get an insight into his view of preaching from a letter he wrote to Jaime Cazador, a Barcelona churchman.

> Concerning the desire you manifest of seeing me in Barcelona and hearing me preach, be assured that I find the same desire in my own heart. Not that I find any satisfaction in doing what others cannot do or in repeating the success of others; but I should like to preach in a minor capacity on subjects that are more easily understood and of less importance, with the hope in God our Lord that, if I take up these humble subjects, He would add His grace so that in some way I might be able to advance in the praise and service I owe Him.[8]

He evidently never saw himself as a conventional preacher even in his native Spain. As it turned out he spent few hours of his priestly life in the pulpit. Besides the administration of what finally became the Society of Jesus, his only priestly apostolates were serving the poor, the sick, and prostitutes, and engaging in spiritual conversation.

It was this gift of spiritual conversation that enabled him to win over his first companions in Paris. The first was Pierre Favre. They took an instant liking to one another. Ignatius shared his money and spiritual wisdom with Favre who repaid him by teaching him logic. But after a time they had to make a pact not to engage in spiritual conversation because they were carried away to the point that little time was left for study.[9]

Francis Xavier was a more difficult case. Ignatius had befriended him too and he was grateful. He was also entranced by Ignatius' conversation, but he was bent on an ecclesiastical career, and had no taste for the poor life to which his older countryman was subtly trying to guide him. Ignatius later said he never tackled a tougher customer than Francis, but he finally succeeded by his delicate dealing and the grace of God in changing Xavier into a great apostle.[10]

---

7 G. Schurhammer, S. J., trans. by M. J. Costelloe, S. J., *Francis Xavier: His Life, His Times*, Vol. I, Europe, 1506-1541 (Rome, 1973), p. 361 (hereafter abbreviated as *Francis Xavier*).

8 *LettersIgn*, p. 16.

9 Schurhammer, *Francis Xavier*, I, 236.

10 Ibid., 172n.

In the last twenty-three years of his life Ignatius dealt with many souls, but he never again found two more apt apprentices in the art of dealing with men and ministering the word of God through spiritual conversation. In the early Society these two companions along with Ignatius himself are universally regarded as the best apostles of the conversational word of God.

Right here we ought to explain the extension of this term. Ignatius uses the Spanish verb *conversar* and noun *conversación* and the Latin and Italian cognates in two different senses. The first sense is the more general one of contact with persons. He thus warns against locating the colleges of Modena and Ferrara too far from *la conversatione della città*, that is, he wants them near the center of town where people gather.[11] The same general sense was retained by the English term "converse."

The second and more precise meaning is treating with or talking with someone. He sometimes uses *conversar* and sometimes *tractar*. The English equivalent would be "dealing with people," and this is the translation favored by Ganss. Referring more particularly to words he speaks of the *gracia de hablar* (*gratia sermonis*), the gift of conversation.[12] But the two closely allied concepts of dealing with someone and conversing with someone overlap and in most cases can be used interchangeably since, as we shall see, one of the most important things about spiritual conversations was learning what not to say and what to do before and after.

It was in both senses of spiritual conversation and the divine art of dealing with men that Xavier and Favre excelled. Xavier spent only a short time in Bologna in 1537-1538, but a generation later people there remembered his art in speaking of divine things: "He was a man full of holy desires and much given to prayer.... He spoke little, but with great persuasiveness. He talked of divine things with great devotion, and his words penetrated into the hearts of his hearers and held them fast."[13] Both Nadal and Canisius cited him as one of the best examplars of this art.

11 *EppIgn*, III, 548.
12 *Cons*, [157].
13 Schurhammer, *Francis Xavier*, I, 386.

Favre also won the admiration of his fellows for his gift of dealing with men. Simão Rodrigues wrote that he had never seen anyone like him for talking souls into the kingdom of heaven.

> I never saw anyone who possessed the same rare and pleasant gift of dealing with souls as Father Favre. He had a mysterious gift of winning friends and he gradually and patiently led them along as he got to know them better to a fervent love of God.[14]

Gonçalves da Câmara, an intimate of Ignatius, recalled meeting Favre in 1544:

> While in Madrid I made my confession to him [Favre] and had some long conversations with him. He amazed me. I told myself that there could not possibly be found in the entire world a man more filled with God. So much so that, when I heard him speak afterwards of the preeminence of Father Ignatius above all the other Jesuits, I had to make an act of faith....[15]

Ignatius himself said of Favre: "Pierre could draw water from a rock." It was Favre that he left in charge of his little band of comrades when he had to leave Paris in 1535. Just as spiritual conversation had been the means of bringing them together, it remained the means of keeping them united in charity and purpose. Years later Diego Laynez, one of Ignatius' first companions, reminisced about their life in Paris. He recalled that they made their vows in August of 1534 at Montmartre and every year they renewed their vows and celebrated with a picnic in the open air. "And we used to do the same thing during the year, bringing each our own food and going to eat on certain days to the dwelling first of one, then of another. And this together with frequent visits and spiritual conversations helped us a great deal to persevere."[16]

Each of the early Jesuits learned the art of spiritual conversation from Ignatius, but the most advanced disciples were Favre and Xavier. Perhaps it was their excellence in this apostolate that made them one after the other Ignatius' choice to succeed him as superior general of the newly founded Society

---

14 Ibid., 253n.
15 *Memoriale*, no. 8, in *FN*, I, 531. Da Câmara continues that once he came to know Ignatius Favre seemed in comparison a little child.
16 *FN*, I, 102-105.

of Jesus.[17] In drawing up the Jesuit *Constitutions* he had been careful to specify (in [729]) that the general of the Society should have the art and grace of dealing and conversing with people, and he put "the art of dealing and conversing with men" among the special means for the preservation of the Society ([814]).

17 *FN*, III, 516; IV, 955; Schurhammer, *Francis Xavier*, I, 439n.

Chapter 3

THE STEPS IN SPIRITUAL CONVERSATION

Comparisons are odious and Ignatius was especially opposed to comparisons of saints; but it was predictable that the early Jesuits would give the preeminence in this apostolic gift to their founder, Ignatius.[1] We shall rely therefore principally on Ignatius as we try to synthesize the early Jesuit teaching on this apostolate. Our sources will be: (1) his deeds—as testified by the earliest sources; (2) his teachings in the *Constitutions;* (3) his written instructions to individual Jesuits and groups of Jesuits.

In connection with this last point we should note that Polanco drew up a series of *Industriae* or Counsels on the Apostolate. In preparation for the writing of the Constitutions we know that Polanco got up some working papers on various points which Ignatius could use in his work of composition. The substance of most of these found their way into the text of the Constitutions. But some of them were not used. These are called *Altera Series Industriarum* by the editors of the Monumenta Historica and contain a good treatise on spiritual conversation.[2] This seems to have been both the result and the source of a good number of instructions which Ignatius gave in his letters on this subject, and we can be sure that the meat of Polanco's compendium was from Ignatius himself. For the most part we shall cite them in the form in which Ignatius used them, namely in his letters. We shall also rely on the deeds and doctrines of the two Ignatian disciples most apt in the art of spiritual conversation, namely, Favre and Xavier. We shall thus be following the example of the two fragments on Spiritual

---

1 See, e.g., *Memoriale*, no. 8, *FN*, I, 531; also *FN*, IV, 850n.
2 *PolCompl*, II, 786-788 & 800-804. These counsels are reprinted in *Imagen Ignaciana del Jesuita en los Escritos de Polanco*, ed. Antonio de Aldama, S. J. (Rome, 1975), pp. 77-131. I owe this reference to an unpublished paper on Ignatian conversation by Jean-François Gilmont.

Conversation presented in the Appendices I and II. They agree in every fundamental point with the Ignatian teaching and develop certain points of that teaching in an interesting manner.

1. *Natural endowment*

After starting Part X of the *Constitutions* with a strong expression of the primacy of divine and supernatural means ([812-813]), Ignatius goes on to speak of the natural means to preserve and develop the Society which should be based on this foundation. He only enumerates the following:

> ...the human or acquired means ought to be sought with diligence, especially well-grounded and solid learning, and a method of proposing it to the people by means of sermons, lectures, and the art of dealing and conversing with men.

Ignatius knew that there had to be a certain natural aptitude to learn this art. He instructed Jesuits to be on the lookout for likely recruits for his order. He wanted candidates "suited to be apostolic workers"; that is, young men of some education who were alert and had pleasing personalities.[3] Polanco admitted that the prudence and aptitude for dealing and conversing with men was something a person is born with.

> ...This ability is surely more a natural gift than something to be learned. If a man does not have the natural knack to deal with men he will generally not be a suitable candidate for the Society unless this weakness is copiously compensated by divine grace.[4]

As we see from the *Constitutions*, in this point the art of dealing with men is much like physical appearance. If a candidate did not have a good presence he had to have outstanding virtues or signs of God's favor to be admitted. One of the good signs examiners were to look out for was a "pleasing manner of speech" (*gracia de hablar*).[5] For this reason every candidate for the Society was to be examined orally by means of a conversation ([142]).

---

3 *LettersIgn*, pp. 268-269.
4 *PolCompl*, II, 800; also in Polanco, *Imagen*, p. 112.
5 *Cons*, [157]; see also the cross-references there to [624, 814]. The principle of compensation is stated in [162, 178, 186].

A certain basic natural aptitude for this gift then was necessary because every person in the Society from the lowest to the highest placed was charged to aid his neighbor with spiritual conversation: coadjutor brothers ([115]), scholastics ([349]), those ordained with less intellectual ability ([461]), those sent on important missions ([624]), the procurator-general ([806]), the secretary ([802]), and the general of the Society ([729]).

The provision in [461] is interesting. Ignatius is talking of the Jesuit who does not have outstanding intellectual gifts. The rector of the seminary has to decide how much schooling he can take. Ignatius readily concedes that there might be cases where a man should make less than the full course. But note how he qualifies the minimum. He should know Latin and get enough schooling "as is necessary to hear confessions and deal with his neighbors." This seems to be the minimum one could demand of a Jesuit and for this a certain basis of natural aptitude was demanded.

2. Modesty

On this natural foundation Ignatius wanted to build first of all habits of modesty. This is what he called them. We would say courteous manner or a good presence or poise, but all these terms have a more secular connotation than he wished. For him a certain bearing should characterize Jesuits. We know that before his conversion he was given to swaggering.[6] He knew by experience that the tilt of a man's head and his walk and bearing plus the tone of voice could betray pride or sadness or despair or other internal disorders. He wanted his followers to translate in their external bearing the internal peace and humility that was the fruit of a profound faith and commitment to God.

Even in prayer he put an extraordinary emphasis on bodily posture. He continued the same emphasis in the apostolate. Most of the instructions he wrote for Jesuits contained this subtle mixture of spiritual and physical attitudes. The important thing was to say something to the neighbor by one's physical

6 See ch. 2 of James Brodrick's *St. Ignatius Loyola* (New York, 1956), esp. pp. 45-48.

appearance. He wrote Father Stephen Baroello: "As to exterior posture, expression, and gait, try to observe a becoming modesty.... Men are quick to notice such externals and one should try to be edifying even in these."[7]

Writing to Salmerón, Jay, and Canisius on their way to Germany, he linked up modesty and orthodoxy of faith.[8]

> It will be helpful if you have the reputation, based on fact, of holding sound doctrine, and this not only in respect of the Society but of yourselves personally. This should be with everybody, but especially with the ruler and men of influence. It will be a very great help toward this authority not only to cultivate interior composure, but such as manifests itself exteriorly; namely, in your manner of walking, your gestures, clothing that is becoming, and above all in the circumspection of your speech, the maturity of your counsels, not only in practical matters but in speculative questions as well. This maturity will prevent you from giving your opinion precipitously if the matter is difficult. In such a case take your time to think the matter over, study the question, and even talk it over with others.

Ignatius knew that the Fathers of the Church traditionally linked a swaggering manner with heresy. Gregory Nazianzen knew that Julian, later to be known as the Apostate, was a bad sort the first time he saw him in public.[9] He did not want his own followers to be so judged. Nor did Ignatius want them to go about with a long face or looking sad. He expected the scholastics to show decorum in going to and from their classes.[10]

One of the most characteristic passages that he wrote on the subject was in the part of the *Constitutions* ([250]) dealing with the novices. It can be presented schematically thus:

All should take special care to guard with great diligence
(1) the gates of their senses (especially the eyes, ears, and tongue) from all disorder,
(2) to preserve themselves in peace and true internal humility,

7 *LettersIgn*, p. 158.
8 *LettersIgn*, p. 213.
9 Cassiodorus, *Eccles. Hist.*, VII, 2. Quoted in Alphonsus Rodríguez, S. J. *Practice of Perfection and Christian Virtues*, Vol. II (Chicago, 1929), 10th treatise, ch. 1, p. 107.
10 *Cons*, [349]; *LettersIgn*, p. 441.

(3)   to give an indication of it by silence when it is to be kept;

(1)   when they must speak, by the discretion and edification of their words, the modesty of their countenance,
the maturity of their walk and all their movements,

(2)   without giving any sign of impatience or pride. In
everything they should try and desire to give the
advantage to others, esteeming them all in their hearts
as if better than themselves,

(3)   and showing exteriorly in an unassuming and simple
religious manner, the respect and reverence befitting
each one's state—

(1)   in such a manner that by observing one another they
may grow in devotion,

(2)   and praise God our Lord, whom each should endeavor

(3)   to recognize in his neighbor as in his image.

We can see here the person in himself, in his relation with his
fellow man, and in his relation with God. In each of the triplets
we have the dialectical movement: exterior, interior, result.
From silence we go to speech, from pride to humility, from
good manners to God.[11]

Later on towards the end of his life he would spend a good
deal of time writing out "Rules of Modesty" which had a great
influence on other religious orders. We shall treat of these
later. Suffice it to conclude here that there was an intimate
connection in the mind of Ignatius between "modesty" and
the ministry of spiritual conversation. He expected men to be
attracted to the Jesuit who showed his inner peace by exterior
composure.

3.   Zeal and love for neighbor

Every candidate for the Society had to be a man of desires,
"desirous of all virtue and spiritual perfection...energetic in
whatever enterprise of the divine service they undertake and
zealous for the salvation of souls" (*Cons*, [156]). This zeal is the
next step in the formation of the minister of the conversational
word of God.

11 François Courel, S. J., and François Roustang, S. J., trans. and ed., St. Ignace:
Constitutions de la Compagnie de Jésus (Paris, 1967), II, 126.

Ignatius often speaks of holy desires in this connection. He demands that the candidate for the Society be a man of desires ([101]). The same thing is demanded in a higher measure of formed Jesuits ([638]), rectors of colleges ([424]), and the general of the Society ([790]). He rarely failed to mention zeal and holy desires in his instructions to Jesuits being sent on a mission. By this he means that the apostle must convince himself of the worth and value of the work he is undertaking. Thus he instructs the fathers sent to Germany:

> Your first and greatest asset will be a distrust of self together with a great and magnanimous trust in God. Join to this an ardent desire, enkindled and sustained by obedience and charity, to attain the end proposed. Such a desire will keep the end incessantly before your mind, and cause you also to commend it to God in your sacrifices and prayers and to make use meanwhile of all other opportune means.[12]

To those sent on the missions he writes: "With regard to the work he undertakes he should prefer to all others that for which he is especially sent."[13] Peter Canisius is even more vigorous on this point. In the repetition of his counsels we see his emphasis on a kind of "spiritual psyching up" by the apostle.

> It is not enough to be persuaded that the job in hand is very pleasing to God, of great importance to the Society, very much in the spirit of our vocation....It often happens that we must still arouse in ourselves and really feel a vigorous yearning to give ourselves to the task, placing however our hopes of success not in ourselves, but in the help of our Creator and Redeemer.[14]

The idea, then, is to be convinced of the worth of aiding one's neighbor. This conviction flows not only from general considerations about how each man has been created by God so that we look upon him not taking into account merely external appearances but the fact that he is made in the image of God and won by the blood of Christ, but we must think concretely of the men we are to deal with in this light. *This* man is a temple of the Holy Spirit, *this* man needs my help. From these considerations too flows love for this soul. As Pierre Favre writes:

> In the first place it is necessary that anyone who desires to be serviceable to heretics of the present age should hold them in

12 *LettersIgn*, p. 212.
13 *LettersIgn*, p. 268.
14 See Appendix II, no. 1, on p. 59 below.

great affection and love them very truly, putting out of his heart all thoughts and feelings that tend to their discredit. The next thing he must do is to win their good will and love by friendly dealings and converse on matters about which there is no difference between us, taking care to avoid all controversial subjects that lead to bickering and mutual recriminations. The things that unite us ought to be the first ground of our approach, not the things that keep us apart.[15]

All the early witnesses tell us of how Ignatius' zeal translated itself into a special love for his neighbor. One of the fattest chapters of Ribadeneyra's biography of Ignatius treats of his charity towards others as proven by incidents in his life. Gonçalves da Câmara tells us that he never spoke ill of anyone, even of those whose faults were widely known. It was his constant habit to look rather for the good in a person and he was able to find some even in the most selfish souls.[16]

This was an aspect of the second part of the Society's goal, the aid of souls. Ignatius thought it was scarcely possible to form apostles from men who did not have an ardent love for their fellow men. At the same time he thought that working for others drew a man closer to God. Araoz said:

> Our Father [Ignatius] thought so highly of spiritual conversation in which his sons spoke of our Lord and virtue with their fellow men that he said it was one of the best ways to obtain the special favor of Christ our Lord. He said that zeal (*hambre*) for one's neighbor was a very plain sign of great progress in the Lord.[17]

4. Selection

Even though spiritual conversation is something that can be practiced with greater or less intensity, Ignatius insists on a

15 *MonFabri*, p. 400. Note that Favre's spiritual journal was called by its first editors "Memorial de quelques bons desirs et bonnes pensées du Reverend Père Maître Pierre Favre." The quotation in the text is taken from Favre's famous letter to Laynez on how to deal with heretics. The whole letter is translated on pp. 163-165 of Mary Purcell's *The Quiet Companion* (Dublin, 1970). On Ignatius' esteem for desires see I. Iparraguirre, S. J., "The Ever Youthful and Dynamic Character of Ignatian Spirituality," in *Communications*, no. 1 (1974), pp. 6-8.

16 Ribadeneyra's *Life*, Part V, ch. 2, in *FN*, IV, 758-775; Da Câmara's testimony in *Memoriale*, no. 379, in *FN*, I, 372; see also III, 58-59.

17 *FN*, III, 189.

choice of people with whom we engage in the more serious sort of conversation. It is the same for all Jesuit apostolates: There must be a choice. In the *Constitutions*, [622, d, e], Ignatius discusses the various criteria for such a choice. After some preliminary considerations he sets down the following very characteristically Ignatian principle:

> The more universal the good is, the more it is divine. Therefore preference ought to be given to those persons and places which, through their own improvement, become a cause which can spread the good accomplished to many others who are under their influence or take guidance from them.
>
> For that reason, the spiritual aid which is given to important and public persons ought to be regarded as more important, since it is a more universal good. This is true whether these persons are laymen such as princes, lords, magistrates, or ministers of justice, or whether they are clerics such as prelates. The same also holds true of the spiritual aid which is given to persons distinguished for learning and authority, because of that reason of its being the more universal good.

These principles are spelled out in his instructions to those going on assignment concerning spiritual conversations. The passage in the instruction of 1552 is typical:

> With regard to the neighbor, we must be careful with whom we deal. They should be persons from whom we can expect greater fruit since we cannot deal with all. They should be such as are in greater need, and those in high position who exert an influence because of their learning or their possessions; those who are suited to be apostolic workers, and, generally speaking, all those who if helped will be better able to help others for God's glory.[18]

Ignatius followed this rule in his own life. His spiritual conversations in the beginning of his conversion were mostly with women of the middle and lower classes. Later on he tried to win recruits at Alcalá and Salamanca and even at Paris with little success. Then he met Favre and Xavier and succeeded. For the rest of his life he tried to win recruits. As for the influentials his choice was determined by his circumstances. At Paris most of the influential men he tried to help were professors of theology; at Rome, they tended to be churchmen and statesmen who could help him win a foothold for

---

18 *LettersIgn*, p. 268.

his new order. In his later years he directed his own efforts and those of his sons towards spiritual conversations with those who were able to found a college of the Society. "You will also have to make an effort to win over individuals and benefactors, and talk with them on spiritual things. To help them with special care is something quite proper and acceptable to God, with whose business we are concerned."[19]

Another principle of selection was the welfare of the apostle himself and the greater good of the Church. He warned his sons not to get in over their heads. He also warned them about too great a familiarity with women which could give scandal and endanger the commitment of the apostle himself.[20] He also felt that uneducated young men of his day were not very influential and hence not very promising spiritual prospects.[21]

Right here we should clearly face the criticisms which Ignatius' counsels on selection of fit persons for our apostolates have elicited. They are chiefly two: male chauvinism and social snobbery or at least elitism. Both of these criticisms are very relevant to the social concerns of our age.

In relation to the first we must frankly admit that Ignatius said some rather harsh things about women, especially those not of the highest social class. To take but one example there is his undated letter to the Jesuits of Portugal:

> I would not have any dealing with young women of the common people, except in church or in an open place. On the one hand, they are lightheaded, and whether there be foundation for it or not, it frequently happens that such dealings give rise to evil talk. Such females are in general more inclined to be giddy and inconstant in God's service. After their devotions are over, they not infrequently turn, sometimes to the flesh, sometimes to fatigue. For this reason many allowances have to be made as to their corporal needs.
>
> If I had to deal with women in matters spiritual, it would be with women of birth against whom no breath of evil rumor could arise. Above all, I would not talk with any woman behind closed doors or in remote places. In this way I would avoid all criticism and suspicion.

---

19 *LettersIgn*, p. 248; see also p. 269.
20 *LettersIgn*, p. 158; *MonNad*, IV, 530-531; *EppIgn*, I, 651.
21 *LettersIgn*, p. 442.

22

In all spiritual associations I should try to make one step of progress safely, and prefer this to making a hundred by putting myself in danger or to advance another at the cost of a serious difference of opinion with him, although I might have been right. A scandal, whether it has foundation or not, does us more harm and neutralizes more than half the progress which God our Lord accomplishes through us, especially in times and places such as these.[22]

In the first place, we have to admit that Ignatius was a man of his times. We know that his religious contemporaries had an even dimmer view of women than he had. In the second place, we also have to recognize that religion in southern Europe in those days was more or less an affair of women and children. Ignatius' ambition was to bring into closer union with the Lord and his mystical body not simply women, but men and influential men. He realized that unless he stressed this new perspective his sons would be occupied with those who traditionally frequented churches and sermons, namely, women. He wanted them to think big. In the third place, the Society of Jesus was a new religious order in an age when new things in the religious sphere were suspect. The most damning calumny in an age when reform was in the air was an accusation of sexual immorality, and his sons had to endure frequent accusations of this kind. It was important, therefore, to establish safeguards and to do everything possible to establish and retain the good name of the Society in the matter of sexual propriety.[23]

But the best refutation of the idea that Ignatius was a misogynist who infected his followers with a contempt of women was his own life and practice and that of his first followers. Hugo Rahner in his carefully annotated edition of Ignatius' *Letters to Women* has shown that the saint's first and most enthusiastic followers were women, and that women were among his most loyal and understanding friends throughout his life.[24]

---

22 *LettersIgn*, p. 442.

23 Both Xavier and Codure were slandered in this connection. See Schurhammer, *Francis Xavier*, I, 492, and the comments of Hugo Rahner in his edition of *St. Ignatius Loyola: Letters to Women* (New York, 1960), pp. 14-16.

24 Hugo Rahner, *Letters to Women*, Introduction, pp. 1-26.

As to the difficulty of social snobbery, we should say in general that Ignatius is not guided in his choice of ministries by worldly values but only by the desire for the greater glory of God. We know that in the Formula of the Institute of 1550 he explicitly spelled out "the works of charity" which Jesuits were to perform. Besides the teaching of catechism to children and unlettered persons and the administration of the sacraments, which were included in spiritual ministries, he enumerated the following ministries: reconciling the estranged, serving the sick in hospitals, and ministering to prisoners.

These same works were treated as corporal works of mercy in the *Constitutions*, [650].

> The members will also occupy themselves in corporal works of mercy to the extent that the more important spiritual activities permit and their own energies allow. For example, they can help the sick, especially those in hospitals, by visiting them and by sending others to serve them. They can reconcile the disaffected and do what they can for the poor and for prisoners in the jails, both by their personal work and by getting others to do it. How much of all this is expedient to do will be regulated by the discretion of the superior, who will keep always in view the greater service of God and the universal good.

Ignatius likewise charged the fathers sent to Trent to teach catechism and serve the sick and he gave the same advice to others whom he sent out on assignment.[25] But except in rare cases he does not expect his Jesuits to carry on spiritual conversations with prisoners or the catechized or the people in hospitals. Nor are they fit subjects for the Spiritual Exercises, even of the first week. We have to remember that the common people in the sixteenth century ordinarily had no education nor did they possess the same facility with words that even the uneducated today enjoy in this age of radio and television.

In many cases they would not have understood the Jesuits if they had tried to initiate spiritual conversations with them.[26] The language they understood was the language of deeds and that was what Ignatius prescribed. It is true that he gave these corporal works of mercy a second place to the ministry of the word and the sacraments. It is also true that one reason he

25 *LettersIgn*, pp. 95, 248.
26 *PolCompl*, II, 788; also in Polanco, *Imagen*, pp. 95-96.

ordered his sons to work among the poor was precisely to show people that they were not interested in a life of ease for themselves. Avarice, Ignatius thought, was one of the chief scandals in the Church of his day and the spiritual and corporal works of mercy among the poor were a necessary part of the apostolate of every Jesuit house or mission. He also hoped that this work among the poor would make his men more humble and keep their heads from being turned by the familiarity and confidence they came to enjoy with the influentials of this world.

We should also recognize the fact that he set up no social barrier for the admission of Jesuits. Some of his best recruits were from the lowest ranks of society, the poor, ex-soldiers, peasants, although in his day, as in ours, the richest sources of vocations were the families of middle-class artisans, merchants, and professional men.

He was rigorously pragmatic in his apostolic choices. Even among the students in Jesuit colleges he thought a choice should be made. It would be difficult, he thought, to discourse with the younger boys about spiritual things but the older boys could be brought together to discuss virtue.[27]

5. Knowledge of the person

After one has made the choice of the person or persons whom one wishes to deal with and engage in spiritual conversation, his next step is to get to know them. "It will help to have an exact knowledge of the disposition and character of the men involved, and to consider beforehand all possibilities, especially in matters of importance."[28] This was not an "investigation" such as a social worker or a credit bureau would undertake. It was a matter of keeping one's eyes and ears open. Ignatius must have known something about Francis Xavier and Jerónimo Nadal before he set siege on their souls in his student days at Paris.

Nadal resisted his invitation to a life of greater zeal and devotion for a long time. He was wary of arguing with him.

---

27 *LettersIgn*, p. 246. It should be remembered that some of the students at the Jesuit colleges were under ten years of age.
28 *LettersIgn*, p. 213.

Later on he wrote of Ignatius, "He got to know men so well that he worked wonders with them. It was as if he could peer into a man's soul and when he spoke men had to admit that he knew them better than they knew themselves."[29] According to Da Câmara Ignatius had a real knack of getting to know the feelings and personality of anyone he talked with. After one conversation he knew a man from head to toe.[30]

The apostle must concentrate on a person's good points. If there were not many bright spots in his present life one had to look for something good he had done in the past. During the conversation one had to listen intently. A Jesuit complained about distractions from people who came to converse with him. Ignatius counselled him to say a prayer before and then to give his caller his undivided attention.[31] He told Salmerón and Broët: "Be ready to listen for long periods."[32]

6. Going in by his door

All this knowledge was a preparation for the next and perhaps the most characteristic Ignatian element in the whole ministry of spiritual conversation. He said, "We have to go in our neighbor's door but come out by our door."[33] He meant that one must take one's neighbor where one finds him and adapt our conversation to his interests. He saw this method justified by Paul's words:[34] "I became all things to all men so as to win all to Christ" (1 Cor. 9:22). Thus he instructs Salmerón and Broët:

> In dealing with men of position or influence, if you are to win their affection for the greater glory of God our Lord, look first to their disposition and accommodate yourselves to them. If they are of a lively temper, quick and merry of speech, follow their lead in your dealings with them when you talk of good and

---

29 *MonNad*, V, 833. On Ignatius' early dealings with Nadal see Nadal's autobiography in *MonNad*, I, and the account in Brodrick's *Origin of the Jesuits;* also in Schurhammer, *Francis Xavier*, I, 241-242.

30 *Memoriale*, no. 199, in *FN*, I, 647; see also III, 268.

31 *FN*, III, 430-431.

32 *LettersIgn*, p. 51.

33 See Appendix I, no. 26, on p. 54 below.

34 This is one of Ignatius' favorite Pauline texts. Notice its use in the quotation that follows.

holy things, and do not be too serious, glum, and reserved. If they are shy and retiring, slow to speak, serious and weighty in their talk, use the same manner with them, because such ways will be gratifying to them. "I became all things to all men."

Do not forget that, if one is of a lively disposition and deals with another who is like him, there is very great danger of their failing to come to an agreement if they are not of one spirit. And therefore, if one knows that one is of such a lively disposition, he ought to approach another of similar traits well prepared by self-examination and determined to be patient and not to get out of sorts with him, especially if he knows him to be in poor health. If he is dealing with one of slower temper, there is not so much danger of a disagreement arising from words hastily spoken.

Whenever we wish to win someone over and engage him in the greater service of God our Lord, we should use the same strategy for good which the enemy employs to draw a good soul to evil. He enters through the other's door and comes out his own. He enters with the other by not opposing his ways but by praising them. He acts familiarly with the soul, suggesting some error or illusion under the appearance of good, but which will always be evil. So we with a good purpose can praise or agree with another concerning some particular good thing, dissembling whatever else may be wrong. After thus gaining his confidence, we shall have better success. In this sense we go in with him his way but come out our own.[35]

We have already seen how Favre advised apostles to talk with heretics about things they had in common. Francis Xavier perfectly exemplified this rule. Of him Father Berzé said:

Before I became a priest, I had learned all sorts of tricks and stratagems, and I have used them out here to see whether I could not render to God as much service by them as before I had done Him injury. I do my best to laugh with those who laugh and I try at times to sing with those who are in a mood for singing. When people are in a merry mood I enter into the spirit of their fun, and when they become sad and weep, I follow their example. If anyone would be helped by seeing me dance, I would dance for them. There may be delusion in this...but I comfort myself because I have seen something of the same kind in Father Francis, whose shoe-strings I am unworthy to untie.[36]

Indeed this adaptability and tact was a hallmark of the apostolate of the early Jesuits. In England John Gerard became

---

35 *LettersIgn*, pp. 51-52; see also p. 213.
36 Quoted in James Brodrick, *St. Francis Xavier* (New York, 1952), p. 463.

adept at hawking terms so he could win over members of the English gentry.[37] Gerard's superior, Robert Persons, was legendary for his winning ways and charm. In a way this was the basis for the legend of Jesuit cunning which soon became a feature of European literature. Jesuits seemed to be able to persuade without seeming to argue, as Ignatius himself did.[38] We shall take up this objection later, but right here we should emphasize that in the eyes of Ignatius this charm was a holy gift of God, although founded on natural talents.

The one exception to Ignatius' rule of conforming oneself to the other's taste in the subject matter of conversation was made to cover those cases where the person never wanted to move from light and vain subjects. In that case his practice and counsel was to bring the conversation back to the four last things. If the person wanted help, he would come back. If these things bored him he would look elsewhere for someone to gossip with.[39]

7. Patience and self-control

An important part of this holy gift of conversation consisted in knowing when to listen. Ignatius long before Dale Carnegie and Carl Rogers knew that the best conversationalist is the person who speaks little and the best counselling is client-centered. But to keep silent and listen requires self-control and abnegation. This is the reason why even in an order whose members were to sanctify themselves by helping others there had to be a period of ascesis at the beginning, which was highlighted by the experience of the Spiritual Exercises where one had an experience of Christ in *silence*. Silence and separation marked the whole novitiate experience and was to be a

---

37 John Gerard, *The Autobiography of an Elizabethan*, trans. and ed. by P. Caraman (London, 1951), p. 15. Note that Gerard used his knowledge of hawking to bring his conversation with English gentlemen around to more profitable themes. Father Basset writes, "As far as the Jesuits were concerned, Gerard's greatest achievement...was his marked ability to speak without shyness of spiritual affairs" (*The English Jesuits* [New York, 1968], p. 130).

38 Da Câmara, *Memoriale*, no. 227, in *FN*, I, 659. See also a like testimony on Favre by Simão Rodrigues (cited in *Dictionnaire de Spiritualité*, II, 2215, in the article on "Conversation Spirituelle").

39 *FN*, III, 431.

significant part of the Jesuit's life thereafter. Without this abnegation the apostolate, far from building up the apostle, the neighbor, and the people of God, could do harm to all three.[40]

And so he repeats in his instructions in many different words the counsel he gave to the fathers going to Trent: "Be slow to speak, and only after having first listened quietly, so that you may understand the meanings and leanings and desires of those who speak. You will thus know better when to speak and when to be silent."[41]

This love of silence, even in conversation, will help the apostle avoid faults that would alienate his hearers such as garrulity, contrariousness, contradicting one's interlocutor, and disedifying or vulgar talk. He is to internalize this discipline to the point that even when he is ill his conversations will be just as profitable to those who visit him as they are when he is in good health.[42]

8. Deeds as well as words

Most serious encounters with persons of promise will not be completed in one conversation. Ignatius himself seems to have thought of spiritual conversations as part of a long campaign. We know that his pursuit of Xavier and Nadal lasted for years. He found that in these campaigns deeds were often more moving than words. He himself set down as one of his fundamental principles in the *Spiritual Exercises:* "Love ought to manifest itself in deeds rather than in words."[43] He proved his love for Favre and Xavier by sharing with them the money he had begged and by finding students for them.

With other "clients" he had to take even more extraordinary means. He tried for a good while to persuade a fellow student at Paris to leave off his habits of debauchery. Having failed to move him by words he waded out one night up to

---

40 *LettersIgn*, p. 94.
41 *LettersIgn*, p. 94, also p. 213, and *EppIgn*, III, 630-631.
42 *Cons*, [89]. On faults to be avoided in talking see *LettersIgn*, pp. 158, 440, and *EppIgn*, XII, 674-676, 678-679.
43 *SpEx*, [230]. This is the note to the Contemplation to Attain the Love of God.

his neck into an icy brook near a bridge the man would have to cross on his way to see his paramour; and when the sinner came in sight Ignatius cried out to him, "Go, you poor wretch, to your filthy pleasures! Do you not see God's punishment hanging over your head? I shall do penance here until I have turned God's anger away from you."[44] On another occasion having been unable to persuade a theology professor to make the Spiritual Exercises, Ignatius played a game of billiards with him with a month of each man's life as the stake. Ignatius won and the doctor of theology had to make the full Spiritual Exercises.[45]

Dealing with men for their spiritual profit, therefore, requires a certain amount of resourcefulness in deeds as well as in words. Pierre Favre held that there were three kinds of language, "that of words, that of thoughts, and that of deeds. He used to say that this last, the language spoken by the good example of our actions, was the most effective and the most easily understood of the three."[46]

Ignatius frequently warned his sons never to make promises or commitments that they could not fulfill. They were always to be more generous in deeds than in words. "Whenever possible, see to it that no one goes away from you sad."[47] That was the desired result. How to achieve it was a skill which only long practice in word and deed could teach. In his instructions to Jesuits he contented himself with general advice, "Show your love in truth and in deed by bestowing favors on many, giving them now spiritual assistance and again in exterior works of charity...."[48]

9. Coming out by our door

As we have often said, Ignatius wanted the apostolic end kept firmly in mind in all of his sons' activities. The whole point of the steps we have traced up to now was the greater

44 Schurhammer, *Francis Xavier*, I, 237.
45 Ibid., 238.
46 Da Câmara, *Memoriale*, no. 28.
47 *LettersIgn*, p. 213.
48 *LettersIgn*, p. 212, also p. 248, and *FN*, IV, 894.

glory of God in the most appropriate manner which the person with whom the apostle was dealing could contribute to it. For some the most that could be hoped for was a sense that someone cared about them; for others confession was the goal; for others a rudimentary knowledge of the truths of the faith inculcated by catechism lessons; for others, Spiritual Exercises of the first week; for others, the full Exercises; for others, a vocation to serve God as a priest or religious; for others the foundation of a Jesuit college.

Most persons one dealt with fell into more than one of the above categories. Ignatius saw an intimate connection between spiritual conversation and the Spiritual Exercises, and also between sermons, confessions, spiritual conversations, and the Spiritual Exercises.[49]

Certeau speaks of the trilogy that sums up the Jesuit apostolates: conversation — confession — Exercises. And Giuliani states boldly: "To give the Exercises is nothing else but to replace a spontaneous conversation open to random inspirations of the Spirit with a planned conversation which follows a pattern more or less determined in advance."[50]

Ignatius appreciated the fact that the virtues of the good talker and the good listener rarely coexisted in the same person. It is the good listener who can practice spiritual conversation. Polanco also insists that if a Jesuit does not have the talent for conversation he should not be sent on a mission unless a man with this talent is given to him as a partner.[51] The same idea is expressed in Part VII of the *Constitutions* which deals with missions. In laying down guidelines for the selection of Jesuits for various kids of missions, Ignatius recognizes that different Jesuits are effective with different types of people. Note that in [624, e, f] he seems to think greater skill and learning is required for the ministry of conversation.

> To treat with cultivated persons of talent and learning, those are more suitable who likewise have a special gift of skill and learning. For these persons can be more successful in lectures and conversations.

49 *LettersIgn*, pp. 95, 268.
50 Michel de Certeau, "L'Universalisme Ignatien," *Christus*, no. 50 (1966), p. 178; Maurice Giuliani in *Christus*, no. 10 (1956), 176-177.
51 *PolCompl*, II, 800; also in Polanco, *Imagen*, p. 112.

For the ordinary people, those will generally be most apt who have talent for preaching, hearing confessions, and the like.

But the best solution is to send a team whose members will complement one another. With a preacher should go a listener.

> The number and combination of such laborers who are to be sent should also receive consideration. First of all it would be wise when possible that one member should not be sent alone. At least two should be sent, that thus they may be more helpful to one another in spiritual and bodily matters and also, by distributing among themselves the labors in the service of their neighbor, be more profitable to those to whom they are sent.
>
> And if two set out, it seems that with a preacher or lecturer there could well go another who in confessions and spiritual exercises could gather in the harvest which the speaker prepares for him, and who could aid the speaker by conversations and the other means used in dealing with our fellowmen.[52]

Nadal favored a kind of combination of sermon and spiritual conversation which would result in a communal spiritual conversation. Something like this was at the origin of the Sodality of Our Lady which was founded by John Leunis.[53]

We get the picture of two Jesuits sent to aid souls. One thunders from the pulpit. The other hangs about the door of the church waiting to preach the conversational word of God to those who have been touched by the words of the preacher. He leads those touched on to confession. Some are urged to make the first week of the Spiritual Exercises. A few are prepared for the full Exercises of one month's duration. Here is the Ignatian plan for evangelization.

10. Review and improvement

There is a dynamic element in Ignatian ideas on the apostolate as well as in Ignatian spirituality. Just as he stressed more than previous spiritual masters the notions of review, examination, and growth in one's personal relationship with God, so he also emphasized the same elements in our action for souls. Just as he insisted on repetitions and disputations in the academic exercises of the scholastics, so also he wanted them to be practiced in the ministry of the word during their

52 *Cons*, [624, g, h]. See also Appendix I, no. 27.
53 Appendix I, no. 28.

32

years of training; and he expected the rector of the college to provide and supervise these experiences for his young Jesuit charges:

> The rector ought himself to explain or teach Christian doctrine for forty days. He should also consider which of his subjects should deal with their neighbors inside the house or outside of it, and for what length of time they should do this, in spiritual conversations, conducting exercises, hearing confessions, and also in preaching or lecturing or in teaching Christian doctrine. They should do this work partly to gain practice themselves, especially when they are near the end of their studies, and partly for the fruit which will be reaped by the others within and without the house. After pondering all the factors, the rector should in everything provide what he thinks to be more pleasing to the Divine and Supreme Goodness and for His greater service and glory.[54]

And this training was to be continued on the job.

> Likewise, when one less experienced in the Society's manner of proceeding and of dealing with the neighbor is sent, it seems that he ought to be accompanied by another who has more experience in that procedure, whom he can imitate, with whom he can confer, and from whom he can take counsel in the perplexing matters which he encounters.[55]

The Jesuits sent on missions were told to reflect together on what they had done:

> Take an hour at night in which each can share with the others what has been done that day and discuss plans for the morrow.
>
> We should agree on matters, both past and future, by vote, or in some other way.
>
> One night, let one of you ask the others to correct him in what he may have done amiss. And he who is corrected should make no answers unless he is asked to explain the matter about which he has been corrected. Another night, the second will do likewise. And thus each one in turn, so that all can be helped with greater charity and will enjoy better esteem everywhere.
>
> Make resolutions in the morning and twice in the course of the day make the examen.[56]

This same advice is repeated in almost all his letters of instruction.[57]

54 *Cons*, [437].
55 *Cons*, [624, i].
56 *LettersIgn*, p. 96.
57 E.g., *LettersIgn*, pp. 213, 296. Iparraguirre saw Ignatius' desire for growth in

The last means to improve one's spiritual conversation and method of dealing with men was to stay in touch with Old Master, Ignatius himself, by means of frequent and detailed letters. He insisted on this point and frequently gave his sons admonitions and helpful hints about procedure, although he rarely tried to direct the details of their activities from Rome. And he further insisted that the prudence necessary to win all to Christ was something that only could be taught by the Holy Spirit.

> We should make use of a holy prudence in adapting our-selves to all. This prudence will indeed be taught by the unction of the Holy Spirit, but we ourselves can assist it by reflection and careful observation. The above-mentioned examen of conscience could be extended to include this consideration, and it should be made at a fixed hour of the day. Special attention should be given to cases of conscience; and when the solution of these difficulties is not clear in the mind, we should not hazard an answer or solution, but first give it the study and considera-tion it requires. . . . The regard we should have for the head and body of the Society is shown principally by allowing oneself to be directed by the superior and by keeping him informed of what he should know and by obediently obeying the orders he shall give.[58]

The most important thing he gave his sons was encourage-ment. The art of dealing with men was a difficult one to learn. One should never be discouraged, even when progress was slow. Jesuits were encouraged to take heart from the examples of the guardian angels. They tried to look after their human charges, but their godly peace was never disturbed when persons turned away from God or were less than generous with him. This counsel was especially appropriate for the early Jesuits who had a lively devotion to angels in general and guardian angels in particular.[59]

the Lord's service as one of his chief characteristics. See "Youthful and Dyna-mic Character," in *Communications*, no. 1 (1974), pp. 14-17.

58 *LettersIgn*, p. 269. Not all of the early Jesuits gave letter writing the import-ance that Ignatius thought it deserved. See his stern letter to Favre on this point (*LettersIgn*, pp. 62-64), and his firm rejections of Bobadilla's excuses (*LettersIgn*, pp. 72-75).

59 *FN*, IV, 896. Ignatius often compared Jesuit superiors to angels. See Jacques Lewis, *Le gouvernement spirituel* (n.p., 1961), pp. 58-59. On Favre's devotion to the angels see the introduction to Michel de Certeau's edition of Favre's *Memorial* (Paris, 1959), pp. 50-54.

Chapter 4

THE LATER TRADITION OF
SPIRITUAL CONVERSATION

Such was the state of Ignatian doctrine on the conversational word of God and dealing with men at the death of Ignatius. How did the doctrine develop in the centuries that followed? Naturally we can say that with this as with many other key points of Ignatian teaching there was always a danger of the synthesis breaking down. Ignatius had insisted on silence, abnegation, self-control. He had warned that the apostle who got in over his head or ventured into situations beyond his skill could harm himself and others, could contribute not to building up the people of God but to tearing down (*non ad aedificationem sed ad destructionem*).

Nevertheless in his dialectical way of thinking he proposed this apostolate to all his sons of whatever degree or stage of preparation. In general we can say that the second pole of his thought, the value of conversation, was appreciated by Jesuits with consistency throughout four centuries. We can see this in the lives of Jesuit saints and heroes: Bernadine Realino, John Gerard, Miguel Pro, Daniel Lord and many others. As for the official pronouncements of generals and congregations, they rallied rather to the first pole underlining the advantages of silence and the retired life and emphasizing self-control, abnegation, and the Rules of Modesty.

One of the chief difficulties was the Jesuit desire for religious respectability. The figure of Ignatius himself was gradually and subtly altered so that he would better fit the classic image of the saint. His apostolic resourcefulness and originality were toned down. We can see this in the careful preparation and publication of the first biography of the saint by Ribadeneyra. In the first draft he told the story of the man who was making a retreat directed by Ignatius. The retreatant fell into a deep spell of melancholy or *acedia* and Ignatius inquired whether he could do anything to cheer him up. The man replied that he would like Ignatius to sing him some Basque folk songs and dance in the Basque manner. Ignatius acceded to his request and performed so well that the retreatant was cheered up and recovered his good spirits. But this story was omitted from the final version, perhaps because it showed Ignatius in an undignified light in a day when even a cheerful saint like Francis de Sales had to stretch a point to see his way clear to justify dancing even for lay people.[1]

We see another aspect of this anxiety in Olivier Mannaerts' comment on Ribadeneyra's biography. He wanted Ribadeneyra's reporting of Ignatius' desire to do "great things" eliminated because in his day this was interpreted as encouraging Jesuits to mix in politics and affairs of kingdoms.[2] A similar reproach was made to Jesuits who practiced the Ignatian art of dealing with influential men. They were castigated as "cunning," "machiavellian," "schemers," and the like.[3]

These judgments no doubt influenced later Jesuit authorities to emphasize the dangers rather than the opportunities in this apostolate. Thus Alfonso Rodríguez in his classic *Practice of Perfection and Christian Virtues* treats the conversational apostolate in his 10th treatise "On Modesty and Silence," and only does so after he has reviewed the faults one can commit by the tongue, including the telling of jokes. His twelfth chapter is entitled "That we should beware of jocose and ridiculous expressions and saying smart and witty things."[4]

Later on in the seventeenth century there were several Jesuit spiritual writers, notably Jean Crasset, who emphasized the dangers of spiritual conversations.[5] Even though

---

1 *Introduction to the Devout Life*, Part III, ch. 34. St. Francis writes, "I was comforted to read...that the blessed Ignatius of Loyola having been invited to play a game accepted the invitation." He is probably referring to the billiards game mentioned above in fn. 45 of ch. 3. On Ignatius' dance see *FN*, IV, 761n., and Schurhammer, *Francis Xavier*, I, 415-416, n. 55.

2 *FN*, IV, 991.

3 See *Christus*, no. 51 (1966), pp. 346-347, and my *Papist Pamphleteers* (Chicago, 1964), pp. 159-167.

4 Vol. II, pp. 103-162 (Chicago, 1929).

5 *Dictionnaire de Spiritualité*, II, 2213. In some instructions the Ignatian tension

Jesuits continued to use this apostolic means to great advantage and to quote the Ignatian dictum about going in their door but coming out ours, it was to other saints such as Francis de Sales and Philip Neri that the devout apostle looked for inspiration. Francis de Sales had said that one could draw more flies with a teaspoon of honey than with a barrel of vinegar and this excellent statement was appealed to more often by the conversational apostle than any Jesuit dictum.

When the Society's law was condensed into a new codification in the *Epitome* in the 1920's, a good number of the prescriptions of the *Constitutions* concerning spiritual conversation were included. But it may be safely stated that a passage in legal language such as the following failed to convey all the richness of the Ignatian doctrine:

> Let all endeavor to pass the time of recreation in a religious manner, lest the spirit grow tepid with too free conversation and thus become distracted. Therefore, banishing all talk of curious and trivial matters, let them accustom themselves to converse as becomes pious religious, with the result that when they come in contact with externs, their conversation will be such as to give edification to their listeners.[6]

This passage was among the things that Jesuits used to hear read at table twice every year. Another item that they heard was Nadal's list of "things that the brethren should take as the subject of their spiritual talks together." It was really two lists. One was a list of subjects. The other was a list of attitudes to be avoided in their spiritual colloquies. They were cautioned not to be garrulous, irritable, hardheaded, and the like. The idea was for them to learn how to speak naturally and gracefully of spiritual things and to pass their recreations together in a manner at once "religiously agreeable and agreeably religious."[7]

But most Jesuits were unable to put Nadal's list into the proper historical or pastoral context and the true value of the

between the necessary time in solitude for prayer, study, or reflection and the necessary time in the apostolate was preserved. See, e.g., the letter of Father Richard Blount, the first provincial of the English Jesuits, in Henry More's *Historia Missionis* (St. Omers, 1660), pp. 482-494.

6 *Societatis Jesu Constitutiones et Epitome Instituti* (Roma, 1962), no. 228. See also nos. 43, 179, 361, 848.

7 See Appendix III below, pages 68-69.

ministry of spiritual conversation never was truly grasped by most. Manners and terminology had changed greatly since the sixteenth century, especially in two areas which we will now consider more particularly.

1. The Rules of Modesty

One need not be a student of history to realize that the sixteenth century was a rough age. Its manners were violent, its jokes coarse, its tone strident. One can see as much in the plays of Shakespeare or even historical films which make some effort at authenticity. Later on the public looked to the nobility for a good example of gentle and graceful manners, but even in the early seventeenth century Great Britain had a monarch, James I, whose ridiculous bearing and slightly comic carriage were accepted by his subjects as a matter of course.[8]

On the continent a more refined tradition was present, though not dominant. The early Jesuits thought that one of the prime purposes of their schools was to train boys in some elements of etiquette. In fact, the rule books of the students at some of the Jesuit colleges were widely circulated as books of courtesy and politeness.[9] What the Jesuits aimed for was not the manners that would suit one for court, but at least a modicum of solid middle-class courtesy which would enable their students to meet people without being ridiculed for their provincial or country coarseness.

It went without saying then that the Society which accepted novices from all walks of life had to train them also to

8 Of King James I Sir Anthony Weldon wrote,"...He was naturally of a timorous disposition...: his eyes large, ever rolling after any stranger came in his presence...: his tongue was too large for his mouth, which ever made him speak full in the mouth, and made him drink very uncomely, as if eating his drink, which came out into the cup of each side of his mouth: his skin was as soft as taffeta sarsenet, which felt so, because he never washed his hands, only rubb'd his fingers ends slightly with the wet end of a napkin...etc." (*The Court and Character of James I* [1651], p. 177).

9 The rules of politeness and manners that were drawn up for the students of the Jesuit College at La Flèche were expanded into the 17th-century English book *Youth's Behavior*. See my *Introduction to Jesuit Life* (St. Louis, 1976), pp. 127-128.

a certain degree of urbanity. The Jesuits wanted to make their novices gentlemen at least in Newman's sense of a person who does not deliberately give pain to others by his bearing and speech. This is the whole purpose of the Rules of Modesty. It is summarized in the 11th rule: "To sum up, every gesture and movement should be of the type that helps others."[10]

We are coming to appreciate better today the importance of body language and the place of the body in prayer. We accept with equanimity the idea of "charm schools," or Dale Carnegie courses, or lecture series on executive development which teach us what to do with our hands, rules of good grooming, or how to appear poised when we meet people. This is what Ignatius aimed for in the Rules of Modesty.

Generations of Jesuit novices heard earnest exhortations about the importance of these rules and the time and trouble devoted to them by St. Ignatius. Even in the founder's lifetime he complained that they were not taken seriously. "I declare to you that they have cost me prayers and tears repeated more than seven times."[11]

But what could be religiously significant about directions on how to walk and where to put one's hands? Jesuits then as now dichotomized the body and soul in a manner completely foreign to Ignatius' thought. He saw the importance of body language centuries before the term was invented.

Another problem was the term "modesty." Even in Ignatius' day it had lost some of its biblical richness. Today it is thought of in connection with length of women's dresses.[12] But the

---

10 See Appendix IV below, p. 71.

11 Both Da Câmara (*Memoriale*, no. 22-23) and Ribadeneyra (*FN*, IV, 736-739) tell the story of how the fathers in the professed house were at a conference on the subject of these rules when part of the house where they habitually gathered after dinner collapsed. They were thus saved from bodily harm and given a divine sign. See A. Coemans, *Commentary on the Rules*, (El Paso, 1942), pp. 346-347. Gilmont thinks these incidents refer to another set of rules on courtesy composed by St. Ignatius, *Les Ecrits Spirituels des premiers Jésuites* (Rome, 1961), p. 87.

12 See, e.g., the article on modesty in the *New Catholic Encyclopedia* where it is defined as "the moral virtue that moderates and controls the impulse of sexual display in man."

Vulgate uses the Latin term "modestia" to translate some very complex Greek terms. Perhaps the most famous passage is Philippians 4:5, "Let your modesty be known to all men. The Lord is nigh."[13] What the Vulgate Bible translated as "modestia," modern English translations render as "gentleness," "meekness," "honorable," "unselfish," or the like. It is one of that cluster of virtues which Christian tradition has called "the fruits of the Holy Spirit": love, peace, patience, kindness, goodness, faithfulness, generosity, gentleness, and self-control.[14]

What Ignatius was aiming at was an exterior attitude that reflected an interior peace characterized by these virtues. The Fathers of the Church wrote lengthily on this modesty and St. Thomas gave it a key place in his catalogue of virtues. He writes abundantly of all kinds of modesty: modesty of soul, of mind, of body, and modesty in externals. He links modesty to meekness, humility, decency, and many other virtues. His treatise on Christian conversation, its opportunities and dangers, occurs in this part of the *Summa theologiae*.[15]

Perhaps the best description of the medieval idea of modesty with which Ignatius was familiar occurs in a modern commentary on the *Summa*:

> It is extremely difficult to describe the part of modesty in human life; that part is so elusive, intangible, yet so solidly real. Perhaps we could call it "personal graciousness."...It has the serene beauty of unhurried movement, the mysterious penetration of

13 Here in Phil. 4:5, Ignatius' favorite text on "modesty," the Greek term is *to epieikes*, that which is fitting, suitable, fair, moderate (rather than insisting on strict justice). It is an adjectival form of *epieikeia*, which in English writings on moral theology became "epikeia." Interestingly, it was translated as *modestia* in the Latin Vulgate, "unselfish" in the New American Bible, "tolerance" in the Jerusalem Bible, "magnanimity" in the New English Bible, and "moderation" in the Confraternity Version.

14 See Gal. 5:22-23; Col. 3:12-15. The Greek terms translated by the Vulgate as *modestia* and allied forms include *prautes, egkrateia*, and many other rich Pauline terms. Many of these virtues are treated by C. Spicq, O.P., in the second half of his *La Spiritualité Sacerdotale d'après S. Paul* (Paris, 1949).

15 *Summa theologiae*, II-II, QQ. 160-170. Note that modesty is a part of the cardinal virtue of temperance and that humility is a part of modesty in Thomas' scheme. See especially the whole of Question 168, which treats (among other things) the wonderful virtue of *eutrapelia*, the virtue of having a happy turn of mind.

a deep chord of an organ. It becomes almost tangible in the face of a saintly old priest, or the eager unselfishness of a very young nun. Perhaps all this may seem much too figurative to be of great help; but, as a matter of fact, we realize the difficulty in everyday life and, in trying to describe the possessor of modesty, we fall back on such utterly simple statements as "wholesome," or, with very special emphasis, we say "he is *good*."[16]

It helps us understand the importance Ignatius attached to these rules or directives if we think of them as the external signs of "personal graciousness."[17] In general, they stand up fairly well after four centuries. Perhaps the only ones which have become obsolete because of different cultural developments are those dealing with modesty of the eyes (Rules 2, 3, 4). It is still bad form to gawk or to rubberneck but at least in Western society today it is a bad sign when one does not present a clear gaze to the person one is talking to. A person who does not look one in the eye tends to be mistrusted.

The other difficulty about the Rules of Modesty is the kind of affected gravity put on by those who try to put them in practice. This is warned against in the rules themselves (no. 7) where cheerfulness is prescribed as the basic overall attitude.[18] But this brings us to our next point.

2. Humor in the Conversational Apostolate

Another difficulty with spiritual conversation is the changing fashions in humor. One constant note throughout all Ignatius' instructions is the condemnation of sadness. And here again he was very traditional, for one of the dreaded maladies of the spiritual life since the time of the desert fathers had been *acedia*, which was a mixture of melancholy, lassitude, boredom, and apathy.[19] The spiritual writers of the Middle Ages had

---

16 Walter Farrell, O.P., *A Companion to the Summa* (New York, 1953), Vol. III, p. 474.

17 See the new title in Appendix IV, "Rules for External Bearing." Many other religious families adopted these rules as part of their institute under the traditional title, "Rules of Modesty."

18 See Mannaerts' warning in Coemans' *Commentary*, pp. 354-355.

19 There are good articles on *acedia* in the *New Catholic Encyclopedia* and the *Dictionnaire de Spiritualité*. See also Cassian in Helen Waddell, *The Desert Fathers*, pp. 157-160.

41

spilled barrels of ink describing this disease and all agreed that it was a bad thing. It was described in various ways in Latin. In English it became "sloth," one of the seven "sins" called "deadly" or "capital" as being the source of many other sins.

Ignatius was thoroughly acquainted with this spiritual malady and he knew its disastrous effects on zeal and apostolic initiative.[20] He considered sadness, therefore, as disorder of the soul and aimed for the happy medium.

> In dealing with others we should bear ourselves modestly and try not to appear glum or too serious, nor, on the other hand, overcheerful or dissipated, but as the Apostle says, "Let your modesty be known to all men."[21]

But what about a sense of humor? In our own day this is one of the most attractive human qualities and it scarcely seems possible to "go in the neighbor's door" unless one has a modicum of wit or at least an ability to appreciate it in others. Here we would have to distinguish between Ignatius' doctrine and his practice. We rarely read of him telling a funny story but his companions do record some remarks of his that if not humorous are at least whimsical. Thus he used to invite guests to dine in the Jesuit house by asking them if they wanted to do a little penance with him. We know that Ignatius shared in the banter among his first companions concerning some of the more outlandish words and deeds of Bobadilla. Once in a discussion of hypocrites Ignatius remarked jokingly that there were only two hypocrites in the Society: Salmerón and Bobadilla. They were both present and enjoyed the teasing along with Ignatius and the others present.[22]

---

20 *Acedia* or depression seems to have been the affliction of the fathers and scholastics of Coimbra which Ignatius tried to correct in his famous letter of 1547. See *LettersIgn*, pp. 120-130. The famous Father Francisco de Strada was depressed in his later years (see my *Introduction to Jesuit Life*, p. 137). Ignatius himself was generally cheerful, though by nature he tended to be serious and phlegmatic. See Schurhammer, *Francis Xavier*, I, 491, with the fnn. When his spirits were low he liked to hear André des Freux play the clavichord (Da Câmara, *Memoriale*, no. 178).

21 *LettersIgn*, p. 441.

22 Da Câmara, *Memoriale*, nos. 23, 374. Bobadilla evidently liked to be teased. See Schurhammer, *Francis Xavier*, I, 207. There are some joking references to him in Xavier's letter to Laynez of 1541 (ibid., I, 720).

He also was known to tease Benedetto Palmio, who was an excellent preacher, about his ability to attract old ladies to his sermons. Like many good preachers, Palmio had a hearty appetite and a portly figure and Ignatius liked to sit next to him so as to rejoice from the delight he took in his food. Gonçalves da Câmara recounts several humorous stories in his *Memoriale* which were evidently told in Rome at Ignatius' expense. One concerned Gerónimo Otello, a Jesuit whose sermons were popular in Rome, whom Ignatius sent to Sicily in 1553. A short time later Ignatius was celebrating Mass in the Jesuit church. When he came to the Confiteor and was reciting the "mea culpa" an old devout woman behind him shouted out, "You can well say 'mea culpa' because you made Father Otello leave this church."[23]

As for his teaching on the topic, it was simply not possible in the sixteenth century, or for quite awhile after, to recommend to a dedicated Christian that he laugh or encourage others to do so. In the first place, the jokes of the age were almost exclusively concerned with the coarser aspects of human life. With rare exceptions such as Thomas More (and even he did not escape criticism for his lack of gravity),[24] the humorists of the age concentrated on gross topics or made unsubtle fun of venerable men and institutions. They offended either against decency or against charity. We can see this in the very traditional chapter which Rodríguez devotes to the topic of jocose and ridiculous expressions. He quotes as do most writers on the topic the opinion of St. Bernard, "Among men of the world nonsense is simply nonsense. In the mouth of a priest it is blasphemy."[25]

We know that Ignatius was greatly displeased at the witticisms invented by Erasmus ridiculing the Church and religious life.[26] He encouraged his followers to try to bring a modicum of charity into the religious controversy, both written and oral,

---

23 Da Câmara, *Memoriale*, no. 95. There are other examples of Ignatian whimsy recounted by Da Câmara in nos. 192, 276, 302, 327.
24 R. W. Chambers: *Thomas More* (London, 1953), pp. 18, 284-285, 347.
25 10th Treatise, ch. 12, in Vol. 2 (Chicago, 1929), p. 150.
26 He complained that his spirit was chilled by reading Erasmus (see *FN*, IV, 172-175).

of his day; but in this, like his successors, he never enjoyed complete success.

Another objection to jokes and witty conversations generally was that they marked a man as a lightweight. This was true in public life down through the nineteenth century in the Western world and is still true today in other parts of the globe. Thus even though today we consider the wit and wisdom of Abraham Lincoln one of his most endearing qualities, in his own day he was, on account of his homely stories, criticized as a buffoon.

Today a sense of humor and an ability to see the non-serious side of things is regarded as a very attractive quality in a person. The apostle, therefore, who reads the signs of the times should be able to laugh at himself and at others as long as charity and decency are preserved. This should be an essential part of the personal graciousness that characterizes the ministry of spiritual conversation.

SPIRITUAL CONVERSATION FOR
TODAY'S APOSTLE

There is a tendency today to make simple things enormously complex. One example is football. To listen to the explanation of some sports commentators or to read the accounts of some writers football is so complex that only someone with an engineering degree can understand it. In reality, as its most successful practitioners periodically remind us, football is simply a matter of knocking people down, with hands on defense and without on offense.

It is the same in the matter of Church reform. Ignatius of Loyola has the name of being an organizational genius, one of the men who masterminded the Counter-Reformation. As a matter of fact, Ignatius did not like the word reform and used it rarely. When Cardinal Marcello Cervini was elected Pope Marcellus II in 1555 he asked his friend Ignatius to make recommendations to him about the reform of the Church. Ignatius' plan was very simple: "If the pope reformed himself and his house and the Roman cardinals there would be nothing left to do and everything else would follow by itself."[1]

The same plan can be adapted to the reform of a diocese, a parish, a retreat house, a religious community or any other unit of the Church. If more detailed rules were found necessary, they could be found in the four mission letters we have quoted so often above: Ignatius' instructions to Salmerón and Broët as they departed for Ireland in 1541, to Laynez and Salmerón as they departed for the Council of Trent in 1546, to Salmerón, Jay, and Canisius on their way to Ingolstadt in 1549, and the general mission letter of 1552.

---

1 Da Câmara, *Memoriale*, no. 343. The whole subject is fully discussed in Cándido de Dalmases, S. J., "Les Idées de Saint Ignace sur la Réforme Catholique," *Christus*, no. 18 (1958), pp. 239-256.

They are all summed up in the following lines of the instruction of 1552:

> As to the instruments we must use, besides good example and prayer that is full of desires, we must consider whether to make use of confession or spiritual exercises and conversations, or teaching catechism, or lectures, sermons, and so forth.[2]

In a pastoral instruction today that last "and so forth" would be expanded to treat of parish and diocesan organization, finances, ecumenism, the promotion of justice, the liturgy, and a host of other topics.

The Church today is rightly impressed with the enormity and complexity of the task of Church reform, and of evangelization which is the final goal of reform. There is great stress on better preaching, the use of the mass media, and adult education. In a world where there are few institutional and social supports for Christian belief we are desperately searching for a way to spread the Good News of Jesus Christ to all persons.

Nevertheless we should periodically remind ourselves that evangelization is basically very simple. Jesus himself gives us the example. He preached sometimes, but more often he conversed familiarly with people, especially his apostles. The example of Jesus reminds us of one truth that we must always come back to, namely, that the means and instruments of evangelization must conform to the substance of the Good News. Here indeed, if nowhere else, it is true that the medium is the message.

We cannot therefore use the same techniques that business and government use to communicate their messages. We cannot use physical or moral force, or group pressure, or false promises to spread the gospel. We must use the language of persuasion. While proclaiming God's word fearlessly and without apologies we must invite persons and draw them on to embrace that word.

Purveyors of aspirin and political candidates have long known that the best way of selling medicine and politicians is word-of-mouth advertising. The principal use of television,

Two-step Flow

Media

↓

Opinion Leaders

↓

Members of Peer Group

direct-mail campaigns, news paper advertisements, and speeches is to start a word-of-mouth persuasion process. One of the great discoveries in the field of public opinion has been the discovery of the two-step flow.[3] It has been demonstrated by research that most people do not form an opinion on important questions by reading about them in a newspaper, hearing about them on the radio, or watching them aired on television. These presentations simply raise the question for the vast majority of people whose mind is not already firmly made up on the question. They only decide on the stance they will take after consulting a more informed member of their peer group, who has also been exposed to the media presentation.

For example, there is a controversy about the merits of the coach of the local basketball team. The media present the facts of the issue one night. The next day at work during lunch hour a group of men discuss the question. One of the men keeps up on such matters; perhaps he has added prestige because he played basketball in college or was a high-school coach. He is the basketball expert in his peer group. Probably his opinion will be very influential in the stance the other members of the group take on the question.

Or take a religious example. On Sunday all the sermons in the local parish are concerned with abortion. A good number of the parishioners have already made up their minds about the morality of abortion, but most have not thought too much about it. A few days later at a ladies' card party the question comes up. Most of them are members of the parish, but one of them is an opinion leader. She might be a nurse or a health

---

3 The theory of the two-step flow was first enunciated in ch. 16 of *The People's Choice* (1944) by Paul Lazarfeld, Bernard Berelson, and Hazel Gaudet. It is developed more fully in Elihu Katz and Paul Lazarfeld, *Personal Influence* (Glencoe, 1955), ch. 14, pp. 309-320.

47

professional. The group turns naturally to her to find out her opinion. There is a discussion of the pros and cons, but most of the ladies present who came without a definite opinion will adopt that of the unofficial "expert" of her peer group.

This is the phenomenon of the two-step flow. Public pronouncements from the pulpit or the TV studio tend to raise the question which is only resolved for most people after they have discussed it in their own peer group and heard the reaction of the opinion leader in that particular area. Information flows from the media in two steps, first to the opinion leader and second, from the opinion leader to the other members of the peer group. People tend to be more influenced by their friends and acquaintances who share their own experience and this is true in housekeeping, automobile repairing, choice of appliances, political issues, and religious questions.

There is little hope, therefore, to evangelize people from the pulpit or the mass media alone. We have to spread the Good News in small groups. A dedicated Christian who achieves a certain status among his friends by his concern for others, by his professional expertise, or by the good example of his life can have a greater influence among his friends than the most eloquent preacher or the most exquisitely staged TV production

Good sermons and the use of the mass media for evangelization are necessary but not sufficient. Christianity in the final analysis for most people will be spread by word of mouth in a conversational setting. The beauty part of this truth is that every Christian can be a missionary. Every person who has received the Good News can bring it to others.

The ministry of the conversational apostle requires no great capital investment or even a massive organizational effort. It is a means of evangelization open to Christians of every age and condition. Of course, as we pointed out above, the conversational apostle needs many skills and virtues. He or she must have a certain natural quality, modesty, zeal, self-control, active charity and a skill in approaching people. Conversation is not easy, but most zealous Christians have the resources to learn it.

The privileged apostolates of the Jesuit conversationalist are summed up in the Ignatian triad: conversation leading to confession leading to the Spiritual Exercises in a retreat. The conversational tone of confession has been rediscovered in the reformed liturgy of the sacrament of reconciliation. The assembly-line aspect of confession has now given way to an atmosphere that encourages a Christian conversation where priest and penitent pray and counsel together in a more humane and open setting.

As for retreats, we used to speak of "preaching a retreat." With the rise of the personally directed retreat we have come to appreciate that the proper tone in a retreat, even a group retreat, is not that of a preacher but that of the conversationalist. Father de Certeau, along with many other authorities, insists that the Exercises are a spiritual dialogue between the director and the retreatant. The dialogue begins in an encounter; it extends to confession; it continues in the Spiritual Exercises, and it culminates in spiritual direction.

Except for confession all of these activities: spiritual conversation, retreats, and spiritual direction are ministries eminently suited for non-priests, both lay and religious. When Ignatius of Loyola began to give retreats he was a layman. In the history of the Church some of the outstanding spiritual directors have been lay persons, male and female.

An ability to talk naturally and sincerely about God and the gospel is necessary too, both for superiors and non-superiors, in religious orders. For Ignatius the *colloquium* between superior and member is the basic instrument of spiritual government as it is for many other religious families.[4] Experience proves that this sort of spiritual conversation is one of the most difficult. Generally it is scheduled rather than spontaneous and the interlocutors sometimes of necessity are scarcely acquainted on a human level, even though they share a religious ideal. It is extremely difficult for either part of this dialogue to profit from it unless he or she is very adept at the art of spiritual conversation.

Many of the skills of the minister of the conversational word

---

4 This type of spiritual conversation is fully treated in the third part of Darío Restrepo, S. J., *Diàlogo: Comunión en el Espíritu* (Bogotá, 1975); see also James J. Gill, S. J., "A Jesuit's Account of Conscience" in *Studies in the Spirituality of Jesuits*, IX (1977), especially 258-274.

of God come into play in other counselling situations: health counselling, psychological counselling, marriage counselling, and academic counselling. Father William J. Byron maintains that there is an Ignatian way to advise students. It would include most of the elements sketched in our third chapter: modesty, zeal, charity, self-control, patience, knowledge, and review-improvement.

The art of the conversational apostle is essential in many other aspects of the spiritual life. Communal discernment is only the first to come to mind. But perhaps the most important benefit derived from learning how to deal with people about God arises in prayer. St. Ignatius in his *Spiritual Exercises* recommends colloquies at the end of each of his meditations or contemplations. In a colloquy we are to speak to Mary, Christ, the Father "exactly as one friend speaks to another."[5] As Father Robert J. Ochs points out, the reason that our colloquies with God are not nearly colloquial enough is that "our personal relationships themselves have become so bland that we have forgotten exactly how intimate friends do speak to one another."[6]

We can hardly hope to learn to talk to God until we re-discover how to talk to one another. Of course, that effort itself demands prayer. We should pursue conversation on both levels. God will teach us better how to listen to and talk with our friends. And our friends will teach us better how to listen to God and to open our heart to him without self-consciousness or self-seeking.

But prayer as conversation with God is another vast subject. We started out to talk about the apostolate of spiritual conversation. I think we have said enough to indicate the importance of this ministry in an age when the fisher of men must work more often with a line than with a net.

---

5 *Spiritual Exercises*, [54].
6 *God Is More Present than You Think* (New York, 1970), p. 8.

JERONIMO NADAL ON
SPIRITUAL CONVERSATION

Most of the letters and unpublished works of Jerónimo Nadal were issued in the four volumes of *Epistolae et Monumenta P. Hieronymi Nadal* (Madrid, 1898-1905). The greatest modern scholar on Nadal, Miguel Nicolau, published the remaining documents by Nadal in *MonNad*, V, *Commentarii de Instituto Societatis Iesu* (Romae, 1962), vol. 90 in the series *Monumenta Historica Societatis Iesu*.[1]

Among these documents was the Sixth Exhortation of those which were probably written between 1573 and 1576, near the end of his long life. He died in 1580 in his 73rd year. The Sixth Exhortation is edited by Fr. Nicolau, from an autograph text in Latin, on pages 820-865 of *MonNadal*, V. It treats of the various ministries listed in the Formula of the Jesuit Institute. The section translated below is from chapter 4 on "Any Other Ministrations Whatsoever of the Word of God," and runs from page 832 to page 837 in Nicolau's text.

The doctrine is consistent with that sketched in the body of our text. Like all the early Jesuits, Nadal appeals to the examples of Ignatius, Xavier, and Favre. The pun on Favre's name (*"Petrus educit de petra aquam"*) is lost in the third sentence of section 24. In his final paragraph ([28]) Nadal refers to priests meeting at San Girolamo, which is the Oratory of Philip Neri. He also refers (in [29]) to beginnings of the Marian Congregations or Sodalities in the Jesuit colleges.

1 However, mention should be made here of still another volume published later: *Jerónimo Nadal, S. I. Scholia in Constitutiones Societatis Iesu, Edición Crítica, prologo y notas* de Manuel Ruiz Jurado, S. I. Biblioteca teológica Granadina, No. 17. Granada, 1976. This is a critically established text, with a helpful introduction and copious scholarly notes, of an important and long influential work of Nadal which before 1976 had been available only in a text which was rather poor and hard to use, published in Prato, Italy, in 1883.

John Leunis, S.J., is credited with founding this spiritual organization at the Roman College in 1563. This is expounded by J. Wicki, S.J., in *Le Père Jean Leunis, S.J.* (Rome, 1951), pages 26-43.

NADAL'S TEXT, FROM HIS SIXTH EXHORTATION

[Ch. 4]. On "Any Other Ministration Whatsoever of the Word of God"

[22]. It is a great grace in the Church of God, and a high office, to be a minister of God's word; and this is a thing we should try to grasp with heart and mind, brethren. Christ is the infinite Word of God and we are the ministers of this Word, for it is he who sends us, he who teaches us, he who gives our lives meaning, who gives us the grace to receive this message and know that it comes from him. He makes his word work in us and endows our work with the savor of charity and with divine enthusiasm. We cannot plumb the depths of the ministry of the word, we can only begin to grasp its inner meaning by the grace of Christ.

The chief duties of this ministry are sermons and sacred lectures or conferences as we have said above. And yet the whole sense of the ministry of God's word is summed up in our fervent spirit. We cannot grasp the totality of this ministry if we pass over its other aspects. Something similar frequently occurs in Holy Scripture when a part that is to come is anticipated. But what are those aspects of the ministry of the word that we have treated up to now only implicitly?

[23]. The first aspect is private spiritual conversation, which is an excellent method of helping our neighbor. Ignatius used to say that this ministry teaches us important things. What preachers and lecturers proclaim from on high, we ought to try to suggest quietly to individuals. And in this latter ministry there is a greater liberty and effectiveness because one can fit the words to the disposition and reaction of the individual. And if we are men dedicated to Christ we will not fail to win souls with this method, by his grace.

[24]. Pierre Favre, one of the first companions of Ignatius, was one of those apostles who had a special talent in this ministry. He had an extraordinary charm in spiritual conversa-

tion, for Pierre Favre never met a man, no matter how far gone, who was not totally changed by dealing with him. Father Ignatius used to say that Pierre could draw water from a rock.

Another Jesuit who stood out in this ministry was Father Francis Xavier, the apostle of the Indies and Japan. Ignatius himself was one of the best. His burning zeal for souls and his gift of discernment and divine tact enabled him with a few winning words to endear himself to everyone he met. He got to know men so well that he worked wonders with them. It was as if he could peer into a man's soul; and when he spoke men had to admit that he knew them better than they knew themselves. On top of all this there was a kind of heavenly glow about him when he spoke of the things of God, which had a striking effect on those present.

[25]. Ignatius was able to do great things through this ministry of God's word. First of all, it was this gift that enabled him to recruit his first nine companions. In some cases this ministry requires more skill than preaching. And yet it is the special quality of the conversational apostle quietly and slowly to win over his neighbor, to deal with him gently and light the flame of charity in his heart. Let me tell you what I know about this ministry from Father Ignatius himself.

What I will tell you he taught not only by word, but also by example. The first thing to do is to concentrate one's heart and soul in loving the person you want to aid. Even though the person in question was a hardened sinner, he found something in him to love, his natural gifts, his belief in God, and any other good things about him. He would concentrate on these things, on his good works, or—in the case of necessity—on the good works he did in the past; and he would point them out to others and discourse on them lovingly. He would test his zeal for the salvation of this soul against all the factors tending in the other direction, especially the evil spirit, who is the source and cause of all vices. He thought one should find out everything possible about the person, his present and past station in life, his intelligence, his physical makeup, his temperament whether it was choleric, phlegmatic, sanguine or melancholy, his past and present deeds. He inquired about all these things so that he could anticipate his needs and disposition.

He further insisted that at the beginning of the encounter there be no talk of sins to be avoided or virtues to be acquired. Rather the conversation should begin naturally. With a soldier one talks of war, with a merchant about his business, with a noble about government or political affairs of his country, with a clergyman about news of the Church and its government. So one should discuss with a man the things that hold an interest for him or that he wants to talk about, and one should follow his lead even into secular topics as long as the conversation is blameless.

[26]. But in these exchanges one should watch carefully for an occasion to give the conversation a religious turn. Father Ignatius used to speak of this method as "entering by their door so as to come out by our door." He was not in favor of launching forth immediately on virtues and vices, the life of Christ, and the last things, because in this way our hearers never really get interested in what we are saying, but are rendered inattentive by our untimely zeal. And even after we have their attention we should not move directly to the reasons why sin should be shunned, but rather, after chatting about politics and news, we should move onto the deeds of holy men, the life of Christ, his teachings and death, and the various good habits. Only after that should we shift our attention to the detestation of bad habits in general. As for the personal problems of our friend we should wait for him to bring up the subject. Only then can we broach this topic without offense. Father Favre used to say that in some cases the whole matter of a long and detailed discussion of a man's sins should be avoided.

If our friend never broaches the subject of his personal problems one can certainly find an opportunity to urge him to make a good confession, or even a general confession, to frequent the sacraments, to learn more about prayer, and to do works of charity with the motive of serving God. It sometimes happens that a man is frequently in our company and yet never gets to the point where he is willing to talk of the things of God bearing on the salvation of his soul. With such a person the best course is not to waste time on trivia even though that is what he wants to discuss, but to turn the talk to hell, the last judgment, the horrible fate of sinners, and the hidden judgments of God. This will either lead him to a different field of interest or send him away annoyed so that he will not come back to waste our time.

[27]. These are but a few hints. There are no hard and fast rules. Circumstances of time and place, and the character and temperament of the person involved, might indicate another approach. The resourceful apostle will be guided by a holy tact in all his conversations.

This ministry is especially helpful after sermons or religious conferences, when good aspirations have been planted in the minds of the hearers and they are ready to listen to spiritual considerations and profit from them.

Spiritual conversation is also very useful in our schools. Both priests and non-priests who have this gift of talking of godly things can lead our students not only to a more intense life with God, but even plant the seed of a Jesuit vocation in the souls of selected youths.

This ministry is also very useful when we meet men in the street or in public places. It is not difficult to get to know them and gradually bring them around to go to confession. In Rome excellent results were obtained in this fashion. A brother might meet a merchant from the country who had come to Rome on business and teach him how to examine his conscience and confess his sins and finally persuade him to go to confession.

We should exercise this ministry not only directly, but indirectly; that is, we should urge our penitents and the friends with whom we dialogue to learn the art of spiritual conversation themselves, so that they may help members of their families and household, their friends and relatives. Women can thus aid other women. But we should not urge this ministry for men and women together unless they be marriage partners so as to avoid the least hint of scandal.

[28]. This ministry can also be practiced communally, as a kind of mixture of the sermon and spiritual conference on the one hand and of an individual spiritual dialogue on the other. For example, a group might gather to talk of godly things together with someone presiding. We started something

like this at Messina in Sicily when we started the college there, but in a very rough fashion. Almost every day a few good laymen who used to frequent our confessionals and attend our spiritual conferences would meet in the church. One of them brought a spiritual book which he read while the others listened. Sometimes they would simply discuss holy topics together. I hear that this died out after a time. Later on at Rome there was a group of secular priests dedicated to St. Jerome which did something similar. They would meet in a large room to listen to a short exhortation by one of their number. The speaker was designated by the priest in charge and he could either be a priest attached to the parish or one of the others. When he had finished he sometimes answered questions about the matter presented. Sometimes they prayed together, often for intentions suggested by the times. The meeting would close with a hymn led by the singer among them.

We had a similar setup at the college in Genoa, but I seem to remember that the general had some objection to it. Still it remains our custom in Rome, in both the Roman College and the German College, to organize sodalities among the students, where spiritual colloquies are held with a Jesuit in charge. Certainly I would think that this kind of ministry would be ideal for our houses, especially the professed houses. Naturally we should follow any policies laid down for this apostolate, but I would hope that we could reap a rich harvest for Christ in the future by this means.

ST. PETER CANISIUS ON
SPIRITUAL CONVERSATION

St. Peter Canisius (1521-1597) was born in Nijmegen, Netherlands, and joined the Society in 1543 after meeting Pierre Favre, who mentions him often in his *Memorial* or private spiritual journal. Canisius cites several passages of Favre's *Memorial* in this letter which was written when he was in virtual retirement at the end of a long and fruitful apostolic life. Besides Favre he knew and worked with most of the great Jesuits of the first generation: Ignatius, Nadal, Jay, Salmerón, Borgia, Laynez, and Ribadeneyra.

Though he was occupied most of his life as a teacher, preacher, and superior, he found time to write many books. His greatest success was his *Catechism, Summa doctrinae Christianae*, published in Vienna first in 1555 and later in many editions and revisions. Most of his other works show the same strengths and weaknesses as the letter which follows. He is prolix, distracted, and diffuse, but his fervor shines through all his twists and turns. No attempt has been made to identify all his direct and implicit biblical references.

The original Latin text of the letter runs almost thirty-eight pages (117-154) in Volume VIII of O. Braunsberger's edition of Canisius' *Epistolae et Acta* (8 Volumes, Freiburg-im-Breisgau, 1896-1923). The first chapter translated here constitutes less than a third of the whole letter. Portions of the second part are translated in James Brodrick, *Peter Canisius* (London, 1963), pages 820-821.

T E X T

Peter Canisius to Claudio Aquaviva   January, 1583
"The eternal peace of Christ Jesus"

Dear Reverend Father:

Last month Reverend Father Hoffaeus wrote to me, asking me in the name of Your Paternity to answer, despite my unimportance, the following questions:

1. How can a Jesuit be most effective in dealing with his neighbor?
2. How can we accomplish this not only among Catholics, but even in heretical regions, and especially in Germany?
3. How can the German College be of the greatest use to Germany? and how can its students best carry out their jobs on their return?

These were the questions Father Hoffaeus put to me, though I have divided his first into two in order to make my answer to them clearer and more complete. I beg pardon in advance for my clumsiness, because for the most part I have said too much and passed the limits of prudence, as you and any competent person can plainly see. You have my permission in Christ Jesus our Lord to correct this paper as you see fit.

Chapter 1. The Duty of Ours in Their Contact with Their Neighbor in General

In order to answer these vast and difficult questions and to satisfy the obligations of obedience as well as I am able, I will set down a fundamental principle. Everyone of Ours who has entered the Society should so live therein that he feels in himself a special attraction for Christian charity, joined to a burning zeal for souls which is evident to all whenever an opportunity presents itself. This will always remain our special obligation. In fact we have no other end or objective than this: with the grace of God to pursue not only our own salvation and perfection, but also the salvation and perfection of our neighbor. That is why we are obliged to love all men of all nations without exception, and to be zealous for their salvation in sincere charity, to serve them, and to become all things to everyone, as far as possible, in order to win them to Christ.

58

It is Christ himself, our Lord and Master, who became our way, truth, and life, who urges and spurs us on to this singular love burning with zeal for the salvation of men. The apostles, who followed Christ to become the fishers of men, likewise urge us; as do our first fathers who, under the leadership of blessed Ignatius, in our Society made themselves masters of the art of dealing with men and commended this same splendid and practical art as the thing most characteristic of our Society. Nor is there any doubt that among all other works of mercy and charity this one stands out as something most pleasing to God and his angels, and the one most praised in the Society and of greatest help to others.

I have put these few words inspired by Christian and apostolic love here as an introduction so that Ours may recognize the importance of this subject. Now let us proceed to the main topic.

1.   If you want to work with God, who burns for the salvation of men, in accomplishing that salvation by means of conversation, it is not enough to be persuaded that the job in hand is very pleasing to God, of great importance to the Society, very much in the spirit of our vocation, as we have said above. It often happens that we must still arouse in ourselves and really feel a vigorous yearning to give ourselves to the task, placing however our hopes of success not in ourselves, but in the help of our Creator and Redeemer. As the Psalmist says, "Unless God builds the house they labor in vain who build it."

2.   If you want to help others by your conversations, you should take the means necessary to make yourself an instrument closely joined to God (*instrumentum conjunctum cum Deo*), your Sovereign Creator, and capable of being used by him. These means are a taste for solid virtue and spiritual things, a pure intention to serve God alone, a special familiarity with God in exercises of piety, a sincere zeal for souls, and especially love which ought to burn in the heart of him who wishes to set others on fire. Nothing is truer than Christ's words: "He who abides in me and I in him will bear much fruit." Something which greatly helps in all this is to see God in all things and to raise your spirit to him often, even outside of special times of prayer; to refer to him in everything, including your activities; and to feel a great devotion in action as well as in

59

prayer, as our father Ignatius taught us both in word and example.

3.   In all this there is needed special and frequent recourse to prayer, so that he who sows and he who receives the gospel seed will be helped by the grace of God which prepares, aids, and follows up good actions. Prayer is like showers from heaven that soak and make infertile soil bloom and often cause it to bring forth a heavenly harvest. Thus the apostles, including Paul, join to their preaching insistent prayer; and they urged their faithful to join in the same prayer. For every good and perfect gift comes from the Father of Light. And prayer not only brings results in the apostolate, it also preserves and adds to them and brings them to perfection. "Ask and you shall receive," says Eternal Truth, "so that your joy may be complete."

4.   Among our first fathers Pierre Favre, whose memory is blessed, taught us to call upon not only God for this purpose, but also his saints. Here are his words:

> I wanted to have a good talk with the Dean of Speyer so I could help him by means of the Exercises. While I was looking in prayer for a way to accomplish this seemingly impossible goal, I found consolation such as I never before experienced. It consisted in praying in the following manner. First I prayed to the Father who was the first to draw him, then to the Mother of Jesus, my sovereign. Third, I prayed to his guardian angel, who was his guide and teacher. Fourth, to the men and women saints who like his brothers and sisters had a special spiritual affection for him. To me this seemed to be a good way to become friendly with someone. I then had the idea of saying the Our Father to the first, the Hail Mary to the second, and to the third, *Deus qui miro ordine angelorum*...and to the fourth, *Omnes sancti tui quaesumus Domine*...It seemed to be an essential step in putting someone in a good and holy frame of mind...to maintain a devotion towards his guardian angels, for these latter have a thousand ways to open hearts for us and to fend off the violence and temptation of evil spirits.

This is the method adopted by Favre during his lifetime. He was not an eloquent speaker, but a man who prayed to God and his saints and, in his dealings with men, an apostle who worked wonders.

5.   Let me mention some other devotions used by this

same father which can be of great help to us when we are travelling or dealing with others.

> Many ways of praying occurred to me as I walked through the mountains, fields and vineyards. One can pray for the increase of good things like this, or thank God for them in the place of those who own them, or ask forgiveness for those who are unable to recognize the spiritual meaning of these creatures or who do not know the One who has given all this to them. I likewise used to pray to the patron saints of these different regions. I asked the saints to do what the inhabitants no longer knew how to do, namely, to thank God, to get His forgiveness for their sins, to ask for the graces they needed.

Such pious practices are very worthy of note provided they build in us a greater love of God and his saints. The same thing is true for other methods of prayer that Favre teaches us. They can be used in any kingdom or principality or domain and they are especially useful when we come near or arrive at a city. That is the time he tells us to pray to the angels, archangels, and saints who are best known in the locality, and to ask them to bless our apostolic efforts in that place.

Because of the prayers of Moses and David and Stephen, God gave many important graces to people who otherwise did not deserve them. Emboldened by this same confidence, the patriarch Jacob, after he had beaten the Angel and obtained strength from him, pleaded with tears for his intercession, as Hosea writes. And Joseph with this same confidence prays, "May the angel who has delivered me from all these misfortunes bless these children." And this preparation is even more pleasing to God and his saints in the measure that it is joined to a sincere submission to his will and a warm confidence in his love. We should imitate the Canaanite woman who, even after she wearied the apostles with pleas for her daughter, obtained the favor desired from Christ, and the centurion who obtained the help of Jesus' friends to obtain the favor desired.

6. Let us move on to those defects which the apostle who wishes to help his neighbor must avoid because they are offensive to people and drive them away from us. The offensive things are those words or actions of ours which flow from impulse or an unsettled state of soul, those things, namely, which betray our arrogance or vanity or indicate levity or

boldness or timidity or rudeness or a lack of reserve or pride—in short, whatever is out of harmony with simplicity, moderation, and a mature manner of acting or speaking. Such things are not serious sins, but they often prejudice the good we want to do. Things we blurt out, sentences spoken without reflection, especially when they are contentious or contrary or bitter or concern those absent—this is what hurts people. The same can be said for private conversations, and much more of sermons and conferences, where we treat of the defects of civil or ecclesiastical authorities, or of the visitation of monasteries, or of the reform of the clergy. When we show by our words that we believe every rumor that comes to our ears, or are preoccupied or too curious about political or wordlly affairs, or have set ourselves up to judge severely everyone else instead of being sincerely, though modestly, interested in the common welfare—all this is harmful. There are so many reasons why the Rules of Modesty and other rules were written by our father Ignatius. The neglect of these rules often causes great harm, notably when we fail to observe temperance, modesty, and self-possession at table, or when we neglect to show reserve and to give edification in our speech, or when we forget to maintain a modest facial expression or a poise in our carriage which reflects patience and simplicity.

7. In all this our father was not only an able master, but also a remarkable model in his own behavior. Everyone knows how he always heard the other man out without interrupting him, how he never spoke of the faults of others in his daily conversations even when those faults were known to all, how he took it ill when he heard men blaming and accusing others, and how he was able to find excuses for the faults of others which he heard recounted. It was his constant custom to speak sparsely and with reserve. His compliments were rare and his accusations even rarer. In his words and actions were blended a remarkable prudence and a rare modesty which flowed from a peace of soul which his frequent examinations of conscience rendered more and more tranquil. Even if we cannot share his sincerity, modesty, foresight, solidity and love, at least we can strive in our dealing with men to be "blameless and innocent," "above reproach," and men who "abstain from every form of evil."

8. To deal with others the simplicity of a dove, which consists in never giving offense to anyone or hurting anyone, is not enough; you also need the prudence of a serpent by which you first of all get to know yourself and then your neighbor. It is a foolish doctor who sets out to treat others without first looking after himself and diagnosing his own maladies and correcting his bad health habits. Such a one will rightly hear, "Doctor, cure yourself," especially concerning a disease which is evident to all. It is the part of prudence to know the character, condition, and habits of the man you are dealing with so that you can, like a conscientious doctor, prescribe the needed medicine according to conditions of time and place. We should start with milder remedies, not forgetting that rule of the apostle: "We who are strong ought to bear with the weakness of those who are sick." Father Francis Xavier was one of our most resourceful apostles. He preached the gospel in the East with tremendous success because he knew how to touch the souls even of great sinners. He first of all got to know without any apparent effort the character and personality traits of the men he was dealing with. He praised the man's good traits and aspirations while passing over in silence those he could not approve. Thus he won little by little the man's confidence and friendship and gradually demanded more of him, namely, to break the chains of his vices, to adopt a way of life closer to the path of justice.

Lovingly Xavier persevered in his apostolic nagging leading his neighbor to more and more profound distaste for his old way of life until he was truly and completely sorry for his sins. Xavier thus brought safely into the port of salvation many a human wreck tossed by the waves of perdition. We are in desperate need of many such doctors of life, endowed as was Xavier with apostolic skills both human and divine, men who are ready and willing to deal with the well and the ill, and skillful enough to convert the most hardened sinners to a better life.

9. But prudence is not enough. You need to be sufficiently strong enough in spirit so that whether or not your efforts are blessed with success you will be courageous and persevering. No cold blast of wind must turn you away from a persistent zeal for souls. These winds are human inclinations, sometimes

coming from the flesh and sometimes from the devil, and always growing stronger when they became habits. They blow even well-intentioned apostles from the right course. Not only do they weaken faith, hope, peace, and spiritual joy, but they give rise to fear, pusillanimity, and spiritual boredom. They make apostles lazy and unenthusiastic for the holy work of saving souls. Finally they make them abandon this divine task in disgust.

You must imbibe the spirit of St. Peter and not give the devil his opportunity. He is the great enemy of the fisher of men and we must say to him with the chief of the apostles, "In your name, Jesus, I will put down my net.... The wind and seas obey you...my future is in your hands." I like to compare our duty to those good guardian angels who never give up even in the case of the most sinful men, but who watch day and night over men, including great sinners. Even when it is clear to them that their charge will never give up his sinful ways, they are not angry or impatient. Having done their duty faithfully, they leave the end result to God.

Fishing in the sea of this world does not always fulfill our desires or expectations. The catch is sometimes out of all proportion to the labor expended by an apostle. This will happen to you. Then is the time to rely on that charity which is "patient and kind, which sustains, believes, hopes, endures to the last." Then even the difficulties and the storms will work together for the good of those who love. Then virtue will be made perfect in weakness, and in patience, which is always a part of perfect works, the fruit will become more abundant.

10. Another thing that will be a great source of encouragement for you is to call frequently to mind that you are an agent not only of the superior, but of Christ our Lord. The man on a mission does not rest but faithfully takes care of the interests of his master. He spends all his time and takes advantage of every opportunity to increase the profit and good name of his master. Our father Ignatius wanted this one point to be especially kept in mind by those who worked in the apostolate, that they were travelling legates of Christ our Lord. Therefore they should watch their own comportment and exercise self-control, especially as regards modesty of the eyes. They had

to stay in a locality for the time necessary, regardless of their success or lack thereof. And finally they were charged to keep their spirit lifted above earth, fixed on heaven and united with God. The man who makes his own these instructions and counsels of our father and puts them into practice will surely become a faithful, resourceful, and valuable legate.

Pierre Favre was such a man. He was sent by obedience to many countries leaving behind him everywhere the pleasing fragrance of Christ. According to Paul's rule, he ingratiated himself with his neighbor in order to build up the man's faith. God gave him the gift of bringing forth from the treasure of his heart good things in all his dealings with men, whether during meals, in inns, or even in the courts of princes. He had a way of speaking of spiritual things which held his hearers' attention, even people of the world. He pursued God's business without boring or annoying anyone. But let this winning and resourceful apostle of Christ speak for himself.

> The spirit led me always to find occasions in inns to help people by teaching and good advice. It is most pleasing to Christ and the heavenly court to leave behind a trail of godly conversations through whatever part of the world we happen to pass. Everywhere we must build, plant, and reap the harvest. We have to be at the service of everyone, in every place and every state of life, wherever we happen to be under the providence of the most sublime Master whose workmen we are. Nothing we see or know should be lost to God because Jesus Christ our Lord permits nothing to happen without a reason, even if it be the sight or sound of something or someone.

There was always a reason for each of his journeys, for his looking at a person, for his being at one moment on land and another on the sea, or his being inside or outside, in a crowd or alone, standing or seated, walking, eating, or sleeping. Nothing he did was without a reason. We should not therefore live a single moment without doing good, not even in a chance meeting with someone, and much less in an encounter that one can foresee.

11.   In such a manner does this father propose as a model for the zealous and devoted missionary of Christ not only his own example, but that of Christ our Lord. The missionary must be a servant of the Lord who is devoted to the greater glory of God, who knows not the meaning of idleness, who is

burning with zeal and intent on the task of winning men to God. He must put aside all timidity and self-doubt and go for the interests of Christ, not his own, and that whether he is dealing with many men or a small number. Such was the charge of the Lord Jesus when he gave out the talents to his servants and told them, "Trade with these while I am away." That is, give them back to the Lord not simply with interest, but with profit. Or again, Be faithful in little things so as to be put in charge of more important matters.

I should add too the useful counsels Father Favre gave in view of the human weaknesses and temptations that some feel. "Sometimes on entering an inn or hostel you meet all sorts of men and women, and this sometimes gives rise to sexual fantasies or involuntary fleshly impulses. In such cases it is often good not only to say at the very beginning 'Peace to this house' but also to make it clear that you are a sincere believer intent on God's business. If you start off talking of the things of God to the person you meet, you subtly close the door to temptations and occasions of sin." And he goes on to say, "It is not wise to imitate those religious who deal with men of the world in a worldly fashion, even to the point of using the vain and frivolous language of worldlings and adopting their attitudes. Instead of keeping their companions, they simply bring contempt on the religious profession. You should so behave that no one broaches in your presence his sinful plans or projects."

12.   What about those Jesuits who have not found this knack, this lovable quality, this *savoir faire* which would make them excellent missionaries of Christ and enable them to deal successfully with men for their eternal good? I would urge such men to examine their own lives in order to find out why they have failed to live up to the true Jesuit spirit which St. Peter inculcates: "Make one another a free gift of what is yours, ungrudgingly, sharing with all whatever gift each of you has received....If one of you preaches, let him remember that it is God's message he is uttering." What holds some back from attaining this heavenly gift or exercising it is a kind of bashful pride or human respect. Others almost never feel free to discuss spiritual things even with their close friends, either because they never learned to do so or because of spiritual boredom. They can hardly get out three words of godly

conversation, even when the time and place call for such. I am not speaking here of those forbidden to speak with others, such as novices. Really how sad and pitiful is the condition of those who, having been called to be fishers of men, find themselves to be instead cold fish. Such an attitude runs squarely counter to that rule so characteristic of the Society: "They ought to try to further the greater interior progress of their neighbors by spiritual conversations, by counselling, and exhorting to good works, especially to confession." And there is that other rule which binds us all. "When they have to speak, they must be mindful of modesty and edification, as well in their words, as in the style and manner of speaking."

If someone has the desire to excel in this apostolate, but lacks the gift of dealing with others, which is so helpful to souls and so rightly esteemed in a Jesuit, he should try to learn from others and to imitate their manner and even their words, so that when the occasion presents itself he will be able to be of spiritual aid to his partner in conversation. Such a man can find something worth saying in the back of the Spiritual Exercises, or in the Catechism, in the Scriptures, in secular biographies or histories, or in other spiritual works.

13. Finally, to sum all this up. The man who wishes to aid his neighbor in his dealings and conversations must carefully establish his own priorities. First should be the most pressing tasks and those ordered by superiors. He should know how to start out in humble encounters and gradually work up to more important ones. He should follow the rules of those sent on missions, namely, that we should always strive in the ministries proper to the Society for the greater glory of God and the more effective aid of our neighbor.

I think that is enough and even, I fear, more than enough on the thoughts that occurred to me in answer to your questions about the methods and means to be used in dealing with men.

NADAL'S LIST

General Congregation II of the Society of Jesus in its decree 57 ordered in 1565 that the Instructions of Nadal be sent by Father General to the provincials to serve as a directive without, however, their having the force of law. Among these instructions was the *Catalogus* or list of Nadal on Subjects of Which Ours May Treat in Their Conversations (*In colloquiis Fratrum agendum*), with the list of things to be avoided also attached.

This *Catalogus* is edited in *Monumenta Nadal*, IV, (Madrid, 1905), pages 450-452. The text in *Institutum Societatis Iesu* (Florence, 1893), III, 373-374, has several important variants. The list below follows the Latin text of the *Institutum*. It is taken from *Renovation Reading* (Woodstock, 1931), pages 2-3. There is no author's name attached to this last version. This is the version that was read in the refectory of most Jesuit houses of study during the semiannual triduum which preceded the renovation of vows in these houses. This custom was in force during most of the history of the Society up until a dozen or so years ago.

TEXT

SUBJECTS OF WHICH OURS MAY TALK IN TIME OF RECREATION

1. Of the Life of Christ or of His Saints, of Church History, of the lives and transactions of Ours.

2. Of progress in spirit, perfection and fruits of prayer, of zeal for souls in the conversion of infidels, or of heretics, or reclaiming bad Catholics, or perfecting good ones.

3. Of things heard in sermons or sacred lectures, or in the reading at table.

4. Of the spirit and Institute of the Society, its Constitution, Rules and the grace of vocation, with humility, however, simplicity and devotion in our Lord with a view to perfect observance.

5. Of one's own vocation.

6. Of the virtues, and particularly of those special to Religious, and in accordance with our vocation.

7. Of the contrary vices, except that contrary to chastity.

8. Of God's judgments, and the four last things.

9. Of the miseries of this life, and the risk of such as live in the world, of the security of those that live in the Society; with humility, however, in nothing setting it above other Religious Orders.

10. Of the good that Ours do to others; of the virtues of our Fathers and Brothers, especially if they be dead or absent.

11. Of heretics and infidels of our age, to encourage us to qualify ourselves with virtue and learning to combat them, and to pray for their conversion.

12. Finally, of such things as may edify and unbend the mind,—have little of speculation and much of affection,— are religiously agreeable and agreeably religious.

THINGS TO BE AVOIDED DURING RECREATION

1. Ours should not be singular, solitary, or gloomy.
2. Nor show levity in gesture.
3. Nor be forward.
4. Nor wordy.
5. Nor irascible.
6. Nor contentious or ironical.
7. Nor walk at too quick a pace.
8. Nor be teasing or bitter.
9. Nor indulge in loud talking or laughter.

Appendix IV

THE RULES OF MODESTY

These rules were composed by St. Ignatius in the last two years of his life for the special benefit of the Roman scholastics. They were in force by January of 1555. The original Spanish, Italian, and Latin versions are edited in *Cons*MHSJ, IV, *Regulae Societatis Iesu*, pages 518-523. This is Volume 71 of the series, Monumenta Historica Societatis Iesu.

The text given below is the new English translation published in the 1964 edition of *Brothers' Manual* (Manresa Press, Harlaxton, England), pages 39-41. The traditional English version is found together with an historical commentary in A. Coemans, *Commentary on the Rules* (El Paso, 1942), pages 346-360. The most famous commentary on these rules is that of Olivier Mannaerts, S.J., in his *Exhortationes* (Brussels, 1912). On this work see Jean François Gilmont, S.J., *Les Ecrits Spirituels des Premiers Jésuites* (Rome, 1961), pages 280 ff. On the Rules themselves see Gilmont, ibidem, pages 86-87.

TEXT

RULES FOR EXTERNAL BEARING

1. It may be said in general of the outward behavior of the members of our Society that there should appear in all their actions self-control and humility, combined with religious gravity; in particular, however, the following points are to be observed.

2. The head should not be turned about unrestrainedly, but with deliberation and only when there is need; and when there is no need it should be kept straight and bent slightly forward, but not inclined to either side.

3. The eyes should as a rule be kept lowered, and not raised unduly or allowed to stray here and there.

4. In conversation, especially with people of authority, they should not stare others in the face, but rather keep their eyes slightly lowered.

5. Wrinkling the forehead and still more the nose is a thing to be avoided, so that a calm expression may be an indication of interior calm.

6. The lips should not be kept too tightly shut or too wide apart.

7. The whole expression should show cheerfulness rather than sadness or any other immoderate emotion.

8. The clothes are to be clean and worn in a way that suits a religious.

9. The hands, if not engaged in holding the apparel, should be kept suitably still.

10. The pace should be moderate, without any sign of haste, except in an emergency, and even then dignity should be preserved as far as possible.

11. In a word, every gesture and movement is to be such as will make a good impression on all.

12. When there are several together they should follow the order laid down by the Superior, going to twos or threes.

13. When they have occasion to speak, they should be mindful of moderation and good example both in what they say and the manner and tone in which they say it.